The Keys to the Boardroom

The Keys to the Boardroom

How to get there and how to stay there

Jo Haigh

crimson

The Keys to the Boardroom: How to get there and how to stay there

This edition first published in Great Britain in 2014 by
Crimson Publishing Ltd
The Tramshed
Walcot Street
Bath
BA1 5BB

© Jo Haigh, 2014

British Library Cataloguing in Publication Data
A catalogue record for this book is available from the British Library.

ISBN 978 1 78059 173 5

Typeset by IDSUK (DataConnection) Ltd
Printed and bound in the UK by TJ International Ltd

To RR my BFF

Who took the keys
And threw them back

Contents

Introduction   xi

Chapter 1 The boardroom and directors: What is their
           purpose?   1
           What is a board and why do we have one?   2
           Board structures   4
           The board meeting   6
           The board's reserved powers   8
           Board committees   9
           The director's role and purpose   10
           Boardroom dynamics and good practice   12
           The director appointment process   16
           The director's role in a quoted or public company   18
           The director's role in a small or medium-sized
           business   21
           General duties for all directors   22
           Director duties in a not-for-profit business   23
           The role of the manager   24
           So is it for you?   25

Chapter 2 The legal implications of being a director   27
           A general overview   27
           Today's legal environment   30
           UK company law requirements   31
           Other critical legal duties   36
           Additional legal principles   38
           International perspectives   39
           How to protect yourself   41
           In summary   43

Chapter 3 Getting the job   45
           Getting noticed   46
           How to recognise an opportunity for a board position   52

	The interview	55
	Nearly there!	60
Chapter 4	**What makes a good board?**	**63**
	The personality traits of a director	64
	How to have a great board meeting	68
	Board performance health check	74
	Board improvements	76
	When the lunatics take over the boardroom	78
	Training and qualifications	78
	Coaching and mentoring	80
Chapter 5	**The first 100 days**	**83**
	Director induction	84
	How to make a good early impression	85
	Checklist for the first 100 days	90
Chapter 6	**Office and boardroom politics**	**95**
	Boardroom survival tips	96
	Is it me?	98
	Be positive and don't worry	99
	Don't allow yourself to be attacked	101
	Tips for dealing with difficult people	103
	Handling difficult conversations	106
	Discrimination and how to deal with it	109
	Moving on or moving out	111
	Forewarned is forearmed	114
Chapter 7	**Board improvements and barriers to change**	**115**
	The female perspective	116
	Does a diverse board improve performance?	117
	Barriers to achieving diversity	120
	Making changes	122
	The future	124
	The end of the journey, the start of an adventure	124
Quiz	**So what do you know about the role of a director?**	**127**

Appendices   135
Appendix 1   Types of company director   137
Appendix 2   Types of business status in the UK   139
Appendix 3   The perfect board meeting agenda   143
Appendix 4   Sample board papers   147
Appendix 5   The appointment process   149
Appendix 6   New director checklist   177
Appendix 7   Insurance policy checklist   181
Appendix 8   Sample evaluation questions   183
Appendix 9   Mentoring and director support organisations   185

About the author   189
Acknowledgements   191

Introduction

Being a board director can be hugely rewarding, both personally and financially. A director of a company is responsible for the well-being not only of the company as a corporate entity, but also of its various stakeholders – employees, suppliers, shareholders and customers, all of whom may have different fiscal requirements. Directors' responsibilities cover anything from job retention to price management to ensuring repayment of loans. It is varied, interesting and challenging work that has a tangible, measurable impact on the success of the business as a whole. And even in the current climate, it can be financially rewarding.

So no wonder it is such an aspirational role. The visible perks of being a company director (smart company cars, executive dining rooms and the like) may not be as prevalent now as they were 20 years ago, but the role can still provide prosperity and personal satisfaction beyond the reach of managers and other employees. The director helps decide upon and navigate towards the company's corporate destination. She is, at least in part, master of her own and many other people's destinies.

But, as Winston Churchill famously once said: *"The price of greatness is responsibility."*

Directors should be high-calibre people. They must be sophisticated communicators and have clear and creative judgement. They need to understand all forms of risk management, both internally and externally, and must be financially literate. They need to be able to deal with the stress that the role brings and the inevitable effect on their personal life.

They also need to be able and willing to put up with an unprecedented level of scrutiny. A deluge of corporate scandals in recent years has shone a light on the director's role as never before. The directors of high-profile companies that fail can expect to face not only shareholder and stakeholder anger but trial by media – and, if they are found to have broken the law, whether intentionally or unintentionally, fines, disqualification or sometimes even prison.

I say "intentionally or unintentionally" because, while there have certainly been cases of crooked individuals who knew exactly what they were doing, further down the scale there are directors of small companies who simply do not understand their responsibilities. They don't appreciate that "getting it wrong", from both a governance and a legal perspective, can now mean not only disastrous personal losses but also loss of liberty.

And yet the number of companies registered in the UK continues to grow every year; for each company that fails, several new ones begin to trade, each one with a board of enthusiastic, ambitious directors. For all the reasons outlined above, the boardroom remains as tempting as ever for many people.

So the time is right for a book that sets out in clear, straight-talking language the role and responsibilities of the company director in the twenty-first century. *The Keys to the Boardroom* offers strategies for both reaching the boardroom and shining once you're there. It shows novice and aspirational directors how to protect their business and personal assets, while offering more experienced directors some critical dos and don'ts for what is probably the most challenging corporate governance period ever. Finally, we'll look at how small changes in the boardroom can generate big improvements, and how boards around the world are dealing with diversity.

The book is based on my many years' experience of being a director, both executive and non-executive, of more companies than I can count. Wherever possible I have offered practical solutions to real-life problems that crop up in the boardroom. Sprinkled throughout the text are personal anecdotes that highlight some of the issues I have faced that could affect any director of any company.

I hope you find this book both useful and inspirational. If the boardroom is where you want to be – read on!

Chapter 1

The boardroom and directors

What is their purpose?

"We make a living by what we get, we make a life by what we give."
Sir Winston Churchill

You will be better equipped to succeed on your epic voyage to the boardroom if you have a good understanding of your destination before you embark.

The board of directors and individual directors have what is called joint and several liability, as well as responsibilities that go beyond legal compliance. As we become a truly global economy, these requirements may not always be identical even across the same continent, and they certainly differ across the world. In most jurisdictions, ignorance of the law is rarely an excuse and ignorance of good practice is simply not acceptable. In the last decade, good practice in the boardroom has become known as "good corporate governance".

Any journey is going to be easier to map if we know the destination and perhaps have some knowledge of what we can expect from our fellow passengers and what may be expected from ourselves.

MY OWN EXPERIENCE

My first board meeting, as a finance director of only 23, was, I recall, absolutely terrifying. I had almost certainly the least exciting report and was the purveyor of bad news – never a pleasant role in a management meeting – but in a board meeting when I was seeking to impress, it was a tough challenge.

My fellow directors, with the exception of the founder managing director (MD), were also all new to the role, and we fumbled around the meeting agenda, all feeling much more comfortable in our "management role" – but it was only years later that this uncertainty really registered as an issue.

Partly this was a result of youth – I mean, what was a director supposed to do exactly? I simply wasn't aware that when you first take that seat at the board table your only certainty is your competence as a manager. What I was to discover in the future was that the two roles of manager and director could not be more different.

So let's start at the beginning...

WHAT IS A BOARD AND WHY DO WE HAVE ONE?

A strict definition of a board of directors is *"the governing body of an incorporated business, the members of which are elected entirely by the shareholders"*.

The role of the board is multifaceted, and includes setting strategy, ensuring that there are sufficient resources to deliver the strategy as agreed by the shareholders, and further supporting the management as needed in the implementation of agreed goals and objectives to ensure that stakeholder requirements are met.

In addition, the directors must ensure that the business is legally compliant.

Stakeholders and shareholders are not the same thing.

- A **shareholder** is someone who owns shares in the business. A shareholder may be an individual or a large public concern. This stake in the business is sometimes known as an equity stake.
- A **stakeholder**, on the other hand, is someone who has an interest in the business, either directly or indirectly. For instance, a stakeholder could be a customer, a supplier, an employee or even a local resident whose interests are affected by the business.

Every company in the UK, big or small, must by law have a board of directors. Technically, if not always practically, the board is the ultimate decision-making authority and has substantial legal responsibilities (see Chapter 2).

If you imagine a company to be a yacht, the shareholders are the boat's owners and the board is its captain, setting the route and steering a safe passage.

In the UK, the US and parts of Europe, a business runs with what is termed a **unitary board**, i.e. one board per company. Limited companies must have at least one director, and companies listed on the public stock exchanges must have two directors plus a qualified company secretary. In other parts of Europe, for example in Germany and Holland, it is more common to have a **dual board** structure; this means there is a supervisory board and a management board (more of this below).

Being a member of a board of directors in the UK requires no official qualification and is open to anyone over 16 years old. (This was a change brought about in the Companies Act 2006; prior to this Act, anyone – even a newborn baby – could be a director!) As a result, enthusiastic people may take up directorships without having any idea about the extent of their role, their responsibilities or their legal obligations, which are quite different to those of a manager.

The members of the board are generally elected by the shareholders, who also have the right to remove them. Removal of a director requires what is called an **ordinary resolution**; this is a majority vote of the shareholders who decide to vote. In smaller companies, where it is often the norm for the directors and shareholders to be the same people, it is not uncommon for the board of directors to have the right to appoint and remove directors, to avoid having to call a shareholders' meeting every time a director position is changed.

BOARD STRUCTURES

Board structures are not always the same nationally and internationally (see Chapter 2). In addition, different sizes of companies often have different board formations. By and large UK companies have single (**unitary**) boards. Internationally (and for PLCs in the UK) the trend is now for **dual** boards i.e. an executive board and a supervisory board.

In the US, most boards have more non-executive directors than executive directors; in the UK, France and Italy it tends to be the other way round. In Germany and Austria, where a two-tiered board structure is commonplace, nearly all the directors on the supervisory board are non-executive directors, while those on the management board are executive directors.

In the continuing, and frequent, debates about business performance, there has been a move towards reforming board structures to ensure a majority of non-executive directors. This has certainly been the case in the UK, but mostly only in large companies and particularly in public limited companies (PLCs).

In my experience, boards fail or succeed not because of their structure but because of the personalities and dynamics of the members who sit around the table, the mood in which they enter the room, and their own personal objectives and priorities. A board works well if the chemistry between its members is good – but sometimes that chemistry just isn't there.

This does not mean that the mood of one person can cause the board to fail, but it could cause a particular meeting to fail. If this becomes a regular occurrence, the next meeting may fail, and the next ... and eventually the board may self-destruct.

Dual boards or two-tiered boards

In this type of structure, there are two distinct boards. The first is the supervisory board, which is likely to be made up largely of non-executive directors (i.e. those directors who do not have functional roles in the business). Almost certainly there will also be a chair, whose role is, among other things, to chair the meeting and the board. In addition, the MD of the company, who may have the title chief executive officer (CEO), will probably sit on the supervisory board.

Underneath the supervisory board is what we term the management board. This will probably be comprised solely of executive directors, i.e. those with functional management roles alongside their directorships. These could include the finance director, the operational director and the marketing director, among others. Usually the CEO/MD and the chair will also sit on the management board.

There are various technical reasons for this dual board process, but the main rationale is that the supervisory board supervises and monitors the policies pursued by the management board and advises on strategic matters and corporate objectives. It is usually the duty of the supervisory board to weigh the interests of the company and all its stakeholders.

Unitary boards or single-tiered boards

This type of structure, which is much more common in smaller companies, tends to have a majority of executive directors, perhaps supported by one or more non-executive directors in a more substantial business.

Summary

Whatever type of board structure you choose, the board of directors will oversee and provide policy and guidance on the company's affairs. The board monitors overall corporate performance, the integrity of the company's financial controls and the effectiveness of its legal compliance, enterprise risk and management programmes.

MY OWN EXPERIENCE

Having sat on single and dual boards, I would suggest that a dual board is really only appropriate for a larger organisation. And even in bigger companies, it can slow down critical decision-making. Most businesses in the UK run very small boards – a large number of them have no more than two directors.

THE BOARD MEETING

Many of the activities described above take place on an ongoing daily basis, but it is at the board meeting that formal decisions are taken. The following is a guide to this process.

One of the toughest jobs for directors new to the role – and even for some well-established directors – is grasping the difference between a board meeting and a management meeting. In fact, when I have challenged colleagues, and indeed delegates at training events on boardroom behaviour, many directors have freely admitted that their "board meetings" are not really board meetings at all.

One tip is to think of them in this way. The purpose of the board meeting is to set the direction of the company, provide leadership, monitor management and support the management process. The management meeting's role is to manage the implementation of board decisions and recommend decisions for approval by the board if any problems are arising.

In other words, the board meeting sets the route to the destination and keeps checking that the company is still on that route and has sufficient resources, while the management meeting is concerned with implementation issues related to getting to the agreed destination. Where confusion arises, it tends to be because directors are much more comfortable debating and discussing management issues rather than strategic ones, as their day jobs are largely in management roles.

In Appendix 3 is a sample board agenda. I devised this after having been in plenty of "bored" meetings that I sought to turn into board meetings.

It is by no means definitive, but people who have used it have found it a good template.

In law, to make a board meeting formal, you require a **quorum**. This is the number of directors who must be present to allow a binding vote to be taken; this number will be laid down in the company's **articles of association**, the contractual document between the company and its directors. The articles of association set out the general procedures that directors must follow in relation to the company, such as how many board meetings are to be held each year and the notice period required for a board meeting.

A set of articles may be unique to the company in question, but they tend to be written very broadly. Therefore, from a good governance point of view, I would suggest that the directors consider the following points in relation to board meetings and, ideally, write them into the articles of association.

1. State that a specific notice period for a board meeting is required, such as five working days (a shorter notice provision for emergencies will be needed and a procedure to deal with this). Most articles say "reasonable notice", which is not easy to determine and, in my opinion, is ambiguous.
2. State clearly those functional titles required for a quorum, i.e. the MD or the finance director. Also, especially if you are an owner–manager, you may like to be certain that you are always in the quorum, or you could risk decisions being taken without you.
3. State that all board meetings must be minuted and those minutes circulated by a given date after the meeting, allowing those not present to know what is going on, and indeed to challenge anything they are not happy with. This is very important, as any director who misses a meeting (if they were sick, for example) needs to know what has been decided in their name, as they will be liable for the consequences of those decisions even if they were not there.
4. State that all meetings must have agendas issued in advance. This stops people hijacking meetings by dropping

"unexpected grenades" into the discussion. It also brings order and creates a sense of priority.

5. State that all meetings should have papers on the relevant agenda items issued in advance. These should, of course, be read by the participants before the meeting. This way you can concentrate on key issues and avoid just going through the motions of reading through yet another boring report.

Of course, while the above are all useful ways of improving a board meeting, most important of all are the individuals around the table and the frame of mind in which they come to the meeting.

THE BOARD'S RESERVED POWERS

This is basically a set of instructions that all directors need to be aware of. They state that no one director can make a decision on the particular areas listed without taking a vote with the rest of the board. This means that critical issues cannot be dealt with by a sole director. Not only does this enable better decision-making but it also protects those directors who may not have been involved in decisions from finding out about an issue too late to do anything about it.

Restrictions on directors' powers can be incorporated into the company's articles of association, but there are two drawbacks to this.

1. If you wish to amend the restrictions you need shareholder approval, which may not always be easy to obtain.
2. The company's articles of association are in the public domain (anyone can look at anyone else's articles).

Therefore, reserved powers are much more effective. They are created and managed by the board, and in addition they form a useful part of any induction programme for directors.

The following is an example of what you may choose to include in the reserved powers. This is by no means an exhaustive list, and these powers should be reviewed at least annually. Possible reserved powers for the board could include:

- approval of press releases
- approval of accounts
- approval of major capital projects (above a specific value)
- remuneration of auditors
- approval of the auditors' engagement letter
- terms of reference for the chair and other directors
- terms and conditions of senior executives
- approval of budgets
- investigation of acquisitions or disposals
- major changes in pension scheme rules.

MY OWN EXPERIENCE

Of all the good governance tools in this book, reserved powers are one of the most effective. They are one of the documents I bring into play (if they are not in use already) as soon as I take up any new post. There is a very simple reason for this.

Imagine a member of your board makes a statement to the press that you would not have approved of had you known about it. As a result, the company is sued and you as a member of the board find you have liabilities for this statement even though you didn't make it (due to joint and several liability, as mentioned earlier in this chapter).

Where a board has reserved powers in place and where such a director has acted outside these powers (for example by talking to the press unilaterally), then the company and the other directors have a right to bring a claim for damages. This is only the case where such powers are in a reserved powers document or in the articles of association. Acting beyond your powers is called acting ultra vires in law – there is more on this in Chapter 2.

BOARD COMMITTEES

As board work can be intensive, sometimes there simply isn't time to get through all the scheduled work in a meeting and, particularly in larger companies, directors may be required to attend various board committees.

Board committees are almost always a prerequisite in a public company and indeed their structure is laid out in the UK Corporate Governance Code (a code of good practice in the UK for PLCs).

Such committees are often established because issues are too complex and/or numerous to be handled by the entire board, or because policies are complex and need expert advice and prolonged debate

There are various types of committee, but the most usual are:

- audit
- nomination
- remuneration
- risk
- health and safety.

These committees improve efficiency and allow more in-depth decisions to be taken, which simply could not happen in a board meeting. They also allow for the provision of expertise and increase independence – critical factors in, for instance, audit, nomination and remuneration decisions.

THE DIRECTOR'S ROLE AND PURPOSE

So if you now have a clearer idea about the board, what is the purpose of the people sitting around the table?

A director, as defined in UK law in the Companies Act 2006, is *"anyone by whatever title they go under who carries out that role"*. Chapter 2 looks at the legal role of a director in detail, but the day-to-day practical role varies enormously depending on whether you're a director of a large multinational, of a not-for-profit company, or of a small owner-managed business.

Overall, the directors' "key purpose", as defined by the Act, is to ensure the company's prosperity by directing the company's affairs and meeting the appropriate interests of its shareholders and stakeholders. In addition to business and financial issues, boards of directors must deal with challenges and issues relating to corporate governance, corporate social responsibility and corporate ethics. They also set strategies, agree vision and values, set company policies, and ensure that the company's objectives are achieved by monitoring and supporting the management team.

However, the formal wording of the Companies Act can seem very far away from the actual everyday role of the director, particularly in smaller companies where directors are involved in the hands-on management of the business from day to day, and where they often lurch from one business issue or crisis to the next.

So although the roles of the manager and the director are different legally in terms of liabilities, they will certainly overlap in smaller organisations. Without a doubt, this can sometimes cause confusion – after all, the owner–manager set up their business not necessarily to design its overall direction but, rather, to engage in the delivery of its services and products. Particularly in the early days, an owner–manager will be heavily involved in management activities and strategic board work is unlikely to be on their immediate agenda. But if you want to be a great director, it is important to understand that members of boards of directors have two roles: one as a joint and equal member of the board, and the other, if you are an executive director, as the head of a function, for example finance, operations or sales.

As a joint and equal member of a board, unless the articles of association say otherwise, each board member has one vote and all decisions are made by a simple majority. This is regardless of executive or non-executive status and in no way relates to numbers of shares held by the directors, at least in theory. (Theory and practice, as we are all aware, can be very different, particularly in smaller companies where the role of director and shareholder can be confused. For example, a board of four directors, three of whom do not own shares, could, in theory, outvote the other director/shareholder on the one vote per director basis. However, if the fourth director owns all the shares, she could then call a shareholders' meeting and, because she owns more than 51% of the shares, remove the directors from the board. Of course, this is not good governance and it may be an extreme case, but even if that person does not take that step, the threat is always there.)

BOARDROOM DYNAMICS AND GOOD PRACTICE

MY OWN EXPERIENCE

I have sat on some great and some disappointing boards, which have included the chair who could silence you with a look, the fellow director who tapped away on his BlackBerry throughout the meeting, and, on the more positive side, the great MD who, despite personal tragedy, held the board together for a successful sale of the business. The chemistry of a good board lies in the mix of its people.

Those who sit around the boardroom table would generally agree that the quality of the interactions between the board members is a critical variable in effective decision-making and in achieving the required outcomes. Choosing the participants around the table with you may be outside your control, but even if you had drawn together your "fantasy board", as a business changes it is entirely possible that what was a great board becomes less effective as the individuals no longer have the necessary skills to deal with new realities.

How directors perform in the boardroom can depend not only on the matter in hand but also on a specific range of personal issues and secret agendas. It is pointless to say you will not be "political" in a board situation; it is akin to saying you won't drink water in a desert. If you aren't political, you simply won't survive. My advice is to act with care, and always to be aware of what is occurring around you.

A great board should contain strong characters and be able to manage challenging decisions. In fact, it has been said that if two people on a board agree, one is unnecessary – although this may be taking the argument a step too far. However, it is important that challenging situations are managed correctly, as excessive conflict means that decisions are never made. Balance is clearly important – but, having said that, Enron was renowned for its good governance!

The fact remains that the dynamics of any board, however good, can be overwhelmed by a dominant CEO or chair. Similarly, it can be made considerably less effective by a board member who is too submissive. There is little point in a director who never voices a criticism for fear of damaging her personal relationships with the other board members. Members of a board are often respected and powerful people and it can be quite uncomfortable for peers to give feedback, particularly if there is something negative to be said.

Defining the role of the directors and the board is vital to maintaining a healthy board. If directors view their role as ambiguous, there is likely to be conflict or withdrawal, so clarity is critical. If directors know where their skills can be used and how far they can go, they will behave and perform better.

As Sir John Harvey-Jones once said: *"The job of the board is all to do with creating momentum, movement, improvement and direction. If the board is not taking the company purposefully into the future – who is?"*

Best boardroom practice

No one thing or one person can make a better board but certain actions and practices can facilitate a smoother and more effective ride. The following are some critical areas to consider.

Be prepared

Nothing is guaranteed to annoy me more than a director turning up at a meeting not having read the board papers. At best this prolongs the meeting unnecessarily; at worst, if the person then fails to properly understand what is being discussed, it can have serious ramifications. If you think papers are being circulated too late to be absorbed properly, or if they're becoming overly burdensome, then you should say so. Don't suffer in silence! If you believe this is an issue, undoubtedly other directors will feel the same way.

Communicate with your management

Management are not mind readers: they need to understand what you want, how you want it and when you want it. They also need to know if you change course and why. So tell them clearly, regularly, and preferably both verbally and in writing to avoid any misunderstanding.

Make decisions

Being a great director is partly about having the courage of your convictions. More and more often, I see procrastination being used as an excuse for not coming to a decision. I am not suggesting unnecessary risk-taking; rather, I am saying that if you are a director, decide on a route and then follow it – and if it doesn't work out, deal with any problems.

Be professional

Unfortunately, many directors develop unnecessarily large egos. Just because you are now in a revered position doesn't mean you should abandon your respect for others. Treat everyone in the manner in which you would like to be treated.

Hidden agendas

On every board I have worked on, one or more of my fellow directors has had a personal plan or goal, sometimes aligned with the business strategy but sometimes not. When this comes to light – as it always does – the outcome is never very positive for the director concerned.

Board dilemmas

Board members are human beings and disagreements are inevitable. If this happens, do not lose sight of the fact that legally you must always act in the best interests of the company and be able to prove this if needed. So you may want to consider how you would deal with the following:

- a company scandal, or a board member who acts illegally
- the needs of an owner or director versus the needs of the company
- a conflict with a supplier who is in some way related to the company owner (e.g. a son supplying goods or services to his father's business)
- an autocratic CEO or owner who is forcing through questionable decisions or possibly a proposal to pay a dividend rather than making an investment in the business.

There is no single "correct" answer to these or indeed any other board dilemmas, but good non-executive directors and strong chairs can help

– unless, of course, they are part of the problem, in which case you may need to consider an external facilitator.

Whatever action you take, you must take action. There is no room for a director who buries her head in the sand, as these matters rarely go away and it is the job of the board as a whole to ensure that they are dealt with swiftly and positively.

Boardroom improvements

In a perfect world, peace and harmony reign and we all work well together. In the real world, this is rarely, if ever, the case and it is unrealistic to believe that your board will not need help from time to time.

Having sat on scores of boards over the course of my career, the following are my own tips for making them run better.

- Don't play games in the boardroom; trust is hard won and easily lost. Sometimes I have been the only person speaking out on an issue, which isn't an easy place to be. However, it is essential to be yourself. As Oscar Wilde reputedly said: *"Be yourself; everyone else is already taken."* Don't be placated by insincere responses, push for honesty. It is your duty as a director.
- Don't bring your personal problems into the boardroom. We all have domestic issues to deal with from time to time, but a director must act professionally and function efficiently at all times. If things are really bad, then make sure your chair knows about it and take some time off.

The board manual

One way to improve your board performance is to have a board manual that formalises board roles, ideals and practices. This is not a mandatory or legal document, but rather a guidebook to good practice in the boardroom. It also helps enormously with director induction.

The contents of the manual are unique to each company and should be updated on an annual basis. However, some things that could be included would be:

- names and mini CVs of the board members
- a sample board paper
- a sample board agenda
- the current business plan
- up-to-date management accounts and forecasts
- copies of the last six months' board minutes
- details of the company's website
- details of all the company's professional advisers
- an organisation chart for the whole business
- copies of the memorandum and articles of association
- various site addresses (if relevant) and contact information.

THE DIRECTOR APPOINTMENT PROCESS

"Never take second best. If you are not happy with the shortlist, then go back in and keep looking. Find people leaving their executive career who are perhaps worrying a bit about what comes next. That requires knowing who, coming out of companies, will be strong on boards."

Phil White, Chairman, Kier Group,
Lookers and Unite Group

Getting the right people around the table in the first place is just as important as the structure of the meeting process. It is also vital for all parties to understand the contractual agreement each director has with the company. This requires sound, clearly understood agreements with all directors – service agreements for executive directors and contracts for services for non-executive directors. (Samples of both types of agreement are available in Appendix 5.) You should always take legal advice on the content of these agreements before signing them. However, the following provides a broad understanding of what they may cover.

Service agreements

These are formal contracts between the company and the executive director that recognise the role of the executive both as a functional head – finance director, for example – and as a member of the board of directors. A service agreement may look like an employment contract but it tends to contain a number of clauses not seen in a standard employment agreement. For instance, it could have extended restrictive covenants; for example, there may be a clause that prevents the director in question working with a competitor for an agreed period after they leave. It may include a "golden handshake" or "golden goodbye" clause, such as the provision of shares to attract the right director, or an enhanced exit package if the position doesn't work out quite as planned. It will cover the details of remuneration and other benefits and will possibly also cover any indemnities or insurance available for the role. Service contracts are usually reviewed at least every three years.

Contract for services

This is an agreement between the company and a non-executive director. Unlike the service agreement discussed above, this is not related to an employment contract in any way, as non-executive directors are generally not employed. However, it usually contains similar basic clauses that cover the agreement between the parties in terms of commitment, time, retention of other roles, length of tenure, how payment will be made, etc. This can be covered in a simple letter of appointment but a more formal contract is preferable.

As a point of principle, it is essential that you have a contract for this role. As Samuel Goldwyn once said: *"A verbal contract isn't worth the paper it's written on."*

General points on appointment

Appointments can be made via headhunters, employment agencies or an internal process. In my experience, the best results come from those appointments that are made on culture, personality and "fit". In fact, I always recruit on enthusiasm and then train the skills, but sadly many appointments are based on age, experience, schools, academic records and just knowing the right people and being in the right place at the right time.

For both parties, the interview process can be confusing, so I usually go to an interview armed with a list of must-haves and should-haves, and hope the interviewer will have the same. Some of these points are considered later in the book, but they should definitely cover the culture of the business and its ethics, values and strategic goals alongside any financial prerequisites you consider essential.

MY OWN EXPERIENCE

I currently sit on the board of a very entrepreneurial business. The owner is charismatic and successful but also something of a control freak. A recent recruitment of a member of the board to a human resources (HR) post went horribly wrong very quickly, as, although the owner in question likes to get his own way, he has no respect for and won't tolerate "yes-men". Such attitudes are, of course, difficult to pick up in an interview, but both sides should have had a clearer understanding of this cultural issue before committing to one another. Indeed, the six-month-long disastrous process left the business with a large headhunter's invoice and a lack of confidence in the recruitment process, and presumably left the candidate with an uncomfortably short appointment listed on his CV.

THE DIRECTOR'S ROLE IN A QUOTED OR PUBLIC COMPANY

The role of a director in a large or public company is very different to that of a director in a smaller business.

A public company must have at least two directors and must hold at least one board meeting a year. Although this is the legal position, most public companies have at least a dozen directors and usually meet monthly for a formal board meeting.

On a public company board, it is very likely that all the main functions will be represented, i.e. finance, sales, HR, marketing and IT operations, along with the MD (or CEO) and a chair. It is also very likely that there will be an equal number of non-executive directors and executive directors and that there will be a dual board process.

Some specific roles at the board table

In a smaller company there has to be one director, who may fulfil a number of functions, whereas in a large company there are more people around the table and they often have very specific roles, as described below.

The chair

Technically, whichever country you are in, there is no such thing as a chair of a company; the role of the chair is always to chair the board of the company. This is largely an ambassadorial and representative role, usually carried out by a non-executive director, who may or may not have a casting vote. Specifically, it may include some or all of the following functions:

- ensuring that the directors (both executive and non-executive) communicate properly
- ensuring good governance
- setting board meeting agendas and running such meetings
- ensuring that relevant board committees are set up, if required
- chairing the annual general meeting (AGM – if applicable, as private companies have not had to have these since the 2006 Act) and extraordinary general meetings (EGMs) as needed.

The managing director or chief executive officer

The chief executive officer (CEO) is the American name for the role more usually called the managing director (MD) in the UK. Technically, a company does not need an MD, or indeed any named functional director, but it is rare not to have anyone in this post except in very small businesses.

If the chair heads the company board, you could say that the MD leads the employees and is often the interface between the board, the employees and other managers. The following functions would come within the MD's responsibility:

- running the business on a day-to-day basis under powers that are officially delegated to her by the rest of the board
- ensuring that the business plan is implemented and that any issues that arise from it are either dealt with or brought to

the attention of the board via the departmental executive directors

- ensuring that the board is fully informed about any operational matters that affect the effective delivery of the company's strategy.

Non-executive directors

These are usually an integral part of a PLC board and bring external independent support and guidance to the business. More and more non-executive directors are being brought in to smaller, privately owned companies; in these cases, their role can be quite different to that of a PLC non-executive director. In a private company, such non-executive directors very often act more like part-time executives and fulfil roles such as that of a finance director where a full-time person is not required. In a PLC, their role is very different and relates more to governance and good board practice.

However, wherever the non-executive director sits, be it in a public or a private boardroom, the legal responsibilities are identical to those of the executive directors on the board.

In my career, I have been both an executive and a non-executive director, in around 40 companies, and I have seen the best and the worst of both roles. The best non-executive directors are those who are totally independent, i.e. they are not dependent on the fees they are being paid and they can remove themselves from operational matters. Actually, in my opinion, I think that having no knowledge of the company's products or services can be really helpful from an operational point of view as it tends to prevent the infamous "we never did it like this at my old place" train of thought.

A good non-executive director should have extensive board experience and ideally a wide variety of business experience, particularly in these challenging times. A few grey hairs and the odd battle scar has helped me deal with some seriously challenging issues.

I never join a board unless I can see what I can immediately bring to it; the last thing I want is any sort of sinecure.

> "When considering a board opportunity, test yourself on what
> you think you can offer. If you join a board where you are able
> to really contribute, you will be valued and enjoy your time."
>
> Stephen Murphy, Former CEO,
> Virgin Group

The senior independent director

Alongside the regular non-executive director, PLCs are required under
the UK Corporate Governance Code to have a senior independent
director. Very often such a person is deputy chair as well, and can also
chair several board committees. In a privately owned company, a senior
independent director would be very rare.

THE DIRECTOR'S ROLE IN A SMALL OR MEDIUM-SIZED BUSINESS

As we have seen already, although the title is the same, the role of a
director in a large multinational is very different to that in a smaller,
owner-managed company.

But whether large or small, all incorporated businesses and directors are
required to comply with the Companies Act 2006, in addition to being
aware of other legislation applicable to them. Regulators and the courts
will not accept the "passive director" as an excuse, no matter what the
size of the company.

The legal duties under the Companies Act 2006 are explained in Chapter
2, as are numerous other legal obligations, but in a small or medium-sized
business (SME) the major practical problem for the director is separating
her role as a director from that of day-to-day management. The board,
if it is formalised, is likely to have a much smaller number of members
than a PLC board, and it is more than likely that all the directors will be
executive directors. It is very unlikely that board committees will exist.

The focus of directors in SMEs tends to be based largely on business
performance along with compliance with the numerous legal obligations
to which both directors and companies are subject. An SME director's
duties may include:

- working side by side with the other directors and managers, not only to set the company's strategy but also to implement it
- working with her team to set budgets (often this may include using an external adviser to support a smaller team if the necessary skills are not available internally)
- dealing with external advisers, including funders, lawyers, accountants, tax advisers and insurance agents
- managing the company's resources – financial management in particular occupies a great deal of the time of many SME MDs.

GENERAL DUTIES FOR ALL DIRECTORS

The duties listed below apply to all directors, whether they sit on a large multinational company board or something more modest, such as a start-up or not-for-profit board.

All directors have financial duties, which include the following. A director must by law:

- keep proper books and records in a format agreed by law
- file accounts annually (nine months after the year end for private companies and seven months after the year end for public companies)
- have the accounts audited if the company fits the threshold, and pay tax as relevant
- ensure that proper insurances are in place.

As well as fulfilling their general financial duties, directors must:

- set up their business correctly at Companies House, registering the name, registered office and registered number
- register the domain name of any website in accordance with various legislation, including the Companies Act 2006
- manage risk and comply with substantial health and safety legislation.

In a smaller company, much of this work will be handled by the MD, possibly with the help of her accountant. In a larger business, such practical activities will not be undertaken by the director herself. However, in both cases the director is the person who will be in the dock, not her advisers, if these matters are not dealt with correctly.

DIRECTOR DUTIES IN A NOT-FOR-PROFIT BUSINESS

In a not-for-profit business, directors (who may also be called governors or trustees) have the same liabilities and responsibilities as those in any other commercial business, but their practical work experience is likely to be very different.

This usually comes as a great surprise to those who take up these posts, often on a voluntary basis. But the responsibilities of a director are the same whether or not the position is paid.

The not-for-profit business in question may be a charity, a housing association or even a school, and the directors may have a mix of paid and unpaid voluntary roles. Although, as the title suggests, these businesses are not there to make a profit to distribute, neither should they make a loss (or they wouldn't survive very long) – their purpose is to make sure that the interests of their stakeholders are met.

The directors of a not-for-profit business are guardians of the company's funds in a way that to some extent goes beyond their role in a traditional commercial company. It could be argued that the directors of these businesses should therefore have a greater financial awareness; they certainly have a duty to ask very probing questions if they do not have such knowledge.

The board structure of such a company is often dual in nature, with a trustee board (most likely comprising non-executive directors and the CEO) and a management board (made up of executive directors). The relationship between these boards is crucial. In particular, the chair and the CEO need to be of a sufficiently high quality, and the relationship between the two sufficiently effective, to act as a catalyst for good performance.

MY OWN EXPERIENCE

These boards can be a good place to start if you want to build your director expertise – but don't assume it will be an easy ride.

Although Wikipedia co-founder Jimmy Wales said *"you should treat your staff like volunteers"*, working on a board largely made up of volunteers can be very difficult politically and emotionally, not to say time-consuming! In my experience, *some* of the decision-making of these directors can be slower than desirable, and *some* of these boards can be more posturing and vulnerable to point-scoring than commercial boards. (Although I stress this is a generalisation – these drawbacks are certainly not unknown in commercial boards!)

THE ROLE OF THE MANAGER

As we have seen, the manager and director roles are legally different but regularly overlap, particularly in smaller companies. However, from a technical point of view, it is worth understanding some specific tasks given to a manager.

The manager in action

A manager has two principal items to consider:

1. the people who report to her and the people she reports to (human resources)
2. the other resources – financial and operational – she has at her disposal.

The manager must implement and achieve the strategic goals provided via the board through the correct allocation and utilisation of these resources.

In order to meet such objectives, the manager's day-to-day role covers a variety of areas, from dealing with personnel matters, for instance a grievance issue from a team member, to negotiating for further physical resources, such as funding for a new piece of equipment.

The skill set a manager needs includes cross-functional communication skills, i.e. the ability to manage discussions and expectations with those who work for her, with those to whom she reports, and also with external parties, such as suppliers and customers.

The stakeholders to whom the manager is responsible may have different priorities, and so a substantial amount of planning will be required to ensure that everything is delivered according to expectations, whether the priority is a product or service or a staffing issue.

The danger for a manager, particularly in a smaller company, is becoming what is known in law as a **shadow director**. A shadow director is a legal director defined in the Companies Act as *"a person in accordance with whose directions or instructions the directors of the company are accustomed to act"*.

Lawyers and accountants acting in their professional capacity cannot by law be shadow directors, unless, of course, they step outside their remit. But it is clear from the above definition that a manager could easily fit into this category. The way to manage this risk is to make sure that the board makes the decisions and the manager acts only within a clear, delegated level of authority.

This is easier in a bigger business, where such lines of authority are clearly set out, but in smaller organisations the lines are blurred at best. If in doubt, always clarify your authority, because if you are found to be a shadow director, you have the same liabilities as any other director.

SO IS IT FOR YOU?

I hope I have not put you off the idea of becoming a director so near the start of this journey, but you should be getting the idea that the role isn't perhaps quite as comfortable as you thought. And the detail of the legal implications is yet to come!

Here is a quick checklist for you to consider when you think about taking a director's role.

1. Do you understand the legal and professional implications of being a director (see Chapter 2 for more details) and are you prepared to accept the risks and challenges involved?
2. Could you read and understand the company books, records, constitutional documents and the latest management accounts? If you cannot do this, you have no right to be applying for or taking up a directorship. You would already be in breach of your duties before you started.
3. Have you seen the business plan and do you understand and agree with the strategy?
4. Are you comfortable with your potential fellow directors, not just professionally but also socially? You need to get on with them. Have you fully checked their credentials? A board is only as good as its weakest link.
5. Have you seen the board minutes and board papers for the last six months? These highly informative documents hold critical information about the quality of decisions made.
6. Have you seen, and are you comfortable with, your service contract in terms of an exit, insurance and restrictive covenants? These can be more or less onerous than employee contracts.
7. Do you have, or does your direct family have, any conflict of interests with the business? Conflicts, although allowable, have to be pre-agreed (see Chapter 2).
8. Have you checked the investment agreement and covenants from funders? If the company in question is in debt, you must be confident that these agreements are being adhered to.
9. Have you seen the risk register and the company's main policy agreements? These could include such things as; health and safety, discrimination, customer care or any number of other processes that a company seeks to adhere to. Are you content that all requirements are being dealt with?

So if you are ready to proceed – read on!

Chapter 2

The legal implications of being a director

"Never let life's hardships disturb you. No one can avoid problems, not even saints or sages."

Nichiren Daishonin

A GENERAL OVERVIEW

MY OWN EXPERIENCE

As you start to read this chapter, you may be surprised or even shocked at the extent of the risk you will be exposed to as a director. I teach good board governance practice to hundreds of people every year. I would guess that 75% of them have no concept of their "risk".

This chapter is not meant to shock you or scare you into choosing a different route, but rather to make you aware of the risks so you can go into the role with your eyes wide open and manage your position as best you can.

The Companies Act 2006 has created the first ever statutory definition in the UK of directors' duties. Historically, directors' duties were to be found in common law (case law), which offered a more subjective approach to the duties of directors. Now the statute gives a very clear and specific set of rules that *must* be followed or the director will be prosecuted.

Directors' liabilities are more onerous than ever before. Depending on the circumstances, a director who fails in her duties can face civil or criminal charges, which at their worst can leave the offender in prison and disqualified from acting as a director for anything between two and 15 years. All types of directors are liable, from public company directors to owner–managers of SMEs.

Your liabilities extend to misleading information that has been put in the public domain that could lead a potential investor to buy shares, even if you did not directly put the information there yourself. Many directors have found themselves in the firing line after the latest corporate scandals, including the former chief executive and chair of Lloyds Bank, yet numbers of director appointments continue to grow.

Although the exposure and risks vary from country to country (this is explained further later in the chapter), your own nationality or domicile is irrelevant. For example, if you are, say, of Chinese nationality, and indeed you live in China, if you join a UK board as the representative director for a Chinese parent company, you become liable under UK law with regard to your UK directorship. Your domicile will not protect you from disqualification if you are found to be non-compliant with UK law.

Insurance against liabilities

It is possible to insure yourself against the possible failings of your fellow directors via **directors' and officers' liability insurance**. This is a policy taken out by the company, if it so chooses, on behalf of the board and the individual directors. It protects any directors who are being sued for breaches, by giving them access to legal insurance costs. However, as with many insurance policies, there are multiple exceptions.

It will not, for example, insure you for unsuccessful claims, nor does it provide insurance against criminal breaches. So your own failings are your own responsibility, and directors' and officers' liability insurance is no panacea. It will not, as one client requested, protect you if you are negligent or fraudulent by accident!

Nevertheless, you should always insist on insurance as part of your appointment and you should also have run-off cover, i.e. the policy should apply for a period after you have stepped down from your directorship. This needs to be a contractual right and not just in the policy itself. You need to have this right in your service contract so that, should your organisation fail to maintain the policy, you will have a breach of contract claim.

The reason why this is important is that your liabilities as a director last forever (subject to certain statutory exceptions such as the statute of limitations) for anything that happened on your watch.

Due diligence

Although technically you have no liabilities for anything that happened before you joined a company, the practicalities of a claim may not be so linear, so before taking up a new post, directors should always undertake their own due diligence.

Here are some of the questions you should have satisfactory answers to before accepting a directorship – however tempting the financial package and other benefits!

- Has the business any outstanding litigation?
- Have you seen the facilities agreements, loans, etc., and is the business in breach of any of its financial covenants?
- What are the company's policies and have you seen them (particularly in relation to risk and to health and safety)?
- Have you seen the latest management accounts?
- Have you read and are you comfortable with the business strategy?
- Have you met your fellow directors and have you seen their CVs?
- Have you any direct or indirect conflicts with the business?
- Are you happy that all relevant insurances are in place, including directors' and officers' liability insurance?
- If there are external shareholders, are you aware of their nature (i.e. institutional or individual) and, if relevant, can you meet them?

- Have you seen the press file and checked out the business's reputation?
- And, most importantly, are you comfortable that you can add value to this board?

TODAY'S LEGAL ENVIRONMENT

MY OWN EXPERIENCE

The law is far from black and white; at best, it's a murky grey. What I mean by that is that it is rarely 100% certain whether an individual is guilty or innocent, but ignorance of the law will never excuse you – forewarned is forearmed.

Some time ago, a client of mine issued a cheque with the name of the company in question spelled incorrectly. When the cheque was returned by the bank because of insufficient funds, my client found himself being pursued for issuing a cheque that wasn't valid, not because of lack of funds but due to the incorrect corporate name, which made him personally liable for the non-payment. His ignorance of this liability was irrelevant.

Your mantra should be: "Look before you leap." It is all too easy to be seduced by the prestige and emoluments attached to the role, but you should take at least a moment to consider some fairly serious issues before you jump in.

Meeting people face to face is, of course, the best way to get information, but there is no shortage of data – and Google provides a substantial insight into most businesses.

Other sources of information include:

- the company report and accounts
- press reports
- the company website
- Experian reports or similar.

Published material is unlikely to reveal any wrongdoing. However, a lack of transparency may be a reason to proceed with caution.

The risks and liabilities apply whether you are a full-time executive or a non-executive director, and all subsequent liabilities are the same even though you could argue that non-executive directors are at a disadvantage with regard to general day-to-day business knowledge. In a litigation situation, this would be irrelevant.

MY OWN EXPERIENCE

For my first directorship, it was definitely the appeal of the title and the new BMW that attracted me. At 23 years old, who wouldn't be tempted? The title, the car, the prestige! Although I had studied law, what you learn in the classroom is not often immediately evidenced in a real-life situation.

I had no real concept at the time of the risks I would be exposing myself to. So take a moment before you sign the engagement terms. It's easier now to look back and go "Oh my goodness, what was I doing?", but it was only when corporate governance became my passion 20 years later that the reality hit me.

UK COMPANY LAW REQUIREMENTS

UK companies and directors are subject to the Companies Act 2006 and to their own articles of association. Other documents that control the authority levels of a director include, but are not limited to, powers reserved for the board, service agreements and delegated authority edicts. However, the main components of directors' duties for UK-regulated companies are set out in the Companies Act 2006. Not fully implemented until 2009, this Act has changed the way in which directors are judged; for the first time ever in UK law, we have a clear set of statutory rules that must be followed.

These rules are listed below. The phrases in quotation marks are taken directly from the Act, but the explanations given should help make them easier to understand.

Duty to act within the company's powers

"A director must:

(a) *act in accordance with the company's constitution, and*

(b) *only exercise powers for the purposes for which they are conferred."*

If a director breached this, it would mean that she was acting **ultra vires** – this is Latin for beyond your powers.

Any activities undertaken by a director which are ultra vires are classed as being the responsibility of the individual perpetrator but all liability for such actions would be attached to that individual and to the company as a whole, including the other directors. However, any directors who suffered because of the breach would have a legal route of redress against the perpetrator.

MY OWN EXPERIENCE

One board member I sat with had spoken at length to the press about a product liability issue – the result was fairly disastrous for the company when the news hit the headlines. The company's articles specifically prevented any director speaking unilaterally to the press, and so the board member had acted ultra vires. As a result, the company was able to successfully bring an action directly against him for the implications of his action.

Duty to promote the success of the company

"A director of a company must act in the way he considers, in good faith, would be most likely to promote the success of the company for the benefit of its members as a whole." A director must, when making decisions (as far as reasonably practicable), consider:

"(a) the likely consequences of any decision in the long term,

(b) *the interests of the company's employees,*

(c) *the need to foster the company's business relationships with suppliers, customers and others,*

(d) the impact of the company's operations on the community and the environment,

(e) the desirability of the company maintaining a reputation for high standards of business conduct, and

(f) the need to act fairly as between members of the company."

Of all the legal duties in the Act, this is probably considered to be one of the most important. It is common for those new to the post of director to think that a director's duty is to put the interests of the shareholders first. In fact, this statutory requirement makes it absolutely clear that when making a decision as a board director you must always do so in such a way as to promote the success of the company. At the same time, you must also consider points (a) to (f) above.

When we discuss the success of the company, it can be useful to think of the company as a person – a legal one, as opposed to a natural one – with their own needs and requirements, some of which may not always coincide with shareholders' needs and requirements. A good example of this would be a shareholder's desire for regular and substantial dividends whereas the company's best interests may require the retention of such payments for investment into other areas such as capital spending.

Clearly, it isn't possible to deliver a positive result for each of these often conflicting groups, but that is not the director's role. You are required to *consider* all of these people and issues, and, if necessary, to prove that you have done so.

Duty to exercise independent judgment

"*A director of a company must exercise independent judgment.*" This means independently from other directors on the board.

Essentially, this means that when you sit at the board table, you should not be unduly influenced by the issues and opinions raised by your fellow directors. Indeed, the decisions you make should always be your own, and, of course, you should always act in the best interests of corporate promotion as set out in the statutory duty mentioned above. If you feel you are being unduly pressured towards one route or another, you should always get appropriate advice.

Duty to exercise reasonable care, skill and diligence

"A director of a company must exercise reasonable care, skill and diligence.

"This means the care, skill and diligence that would be exercised by a reasonably diligent person with:

> *(a) the general knowledge, skill and experience that may reasonably be expected of a person carrying out the functions carried out by the director in relation to the company, and*
>
> *(b) the general knowledge, skill and experience that the director has."*

This largely means that you are not expected to have knowledge or skills beyond those that would be expected of a person reasonably similar to yourself carrying out that role. You are not, in other words, expected to be something you are not.

But do not take this as permission not to be careful. Legally, you must be seen to be doing the best you can at all times, and to ask – and be seen to be asking – for guidance and help.

Duty to avoid conflicts of interest

"A director of a company must avoid a situation in which he has, or can have, a direct or indirect interest that conflicts, or possibly may conflict, with the interests of the company."

This covers all conflicts, actual or potential, between the interests of the director and the interests of the company.

This duty is a "try to avoid" rather than a "you can't do this". It is often impossible not to have a conflict; for example, it is quite common for a director to sit on two company boards, and those two companies may trade with each other. There would clearly be a potential conflict here: you may not be able to fulfil your duty relating to promoting the success of your company for both companies if one were buying from the other, as each would be concerned about getting the best price.

This statutory requirement is about recognising that this situation may occur and agreeing how to behave. Practically, if this does happen, a director should declare this conflict and ideally not participate in the decision being made.

Duty not to accept benefits from third parties

"A director of a company must not accept a benefit from a third party conferred by reason of:

> *(a) his being a director, or*
> *(b) his doing (or not doing) anything as director."*

This duty includes non-financial benefits (for example the appointment of a director to an honorary or non-remunerative position) as well as items with a monetary value. However, it does not prohibit directors from accepting a benefit from a third party if such acceptance cannot reasonably be regarded as likely to give rise to a conflict of interest.

The key here is that the benefit is given *because* the individual is a director. If there is any doubt whatsoever, take advice. However, it may be advisable to explain in board minutes why the proposed acceptance of benefits by a director is not reasonably regarded as likely to give rise to a conflict.

Duty to declare an interest

"If a director of a company is in any way, directly or indirectly, interested in a proposed transaction or arrangement with the company, he must declare the nature and extent of that interest to the other directors."

Such an interest may be where a director rents her own property to the company. Once again, this does not mean that you cannot do this, but, rather, it must be made clear that there is an interest, and indeed that you have permission for this interest to be allowed.

OTHER CRITICAL LEGAL DUTIES

An astute director will have at least a broad understanding of some of the critical legal areas for which she has both responsibilities and liabilities. The following is not an exhaustive list but covers the main areas that any director should be aware of.

Theft and fraud

Although a company cannot easily commit theft, which is a physical act, it can commit fraud. Even if you were not the perpetrator, if you consented to or connived in the fraud, you would be deemed to have committed the offence.

Securities law

This is particularly relevant to directors of companies who sell their shares on the stock exchange. If according to insider trading rules, they *"knowingly or recklessly make a materially misleading, false or deceptive statement, promise or forecast to induce a person to buy or sell shares"*, they will be guilty of market abuse, a criminal offence.

Insolvency

A director can be liable to make good any sums lost by creditors, under what is called a **contribution order**. This means what it says on the tin – you have to contribute to the shortfall the creditors have suffered as a result of your actions, especially if, for example, you allowed, in the words of the Insolvency Act, *"a company to continue trading when you knew or ought to have concluded that it had no reasonable prospect of avoiding insolvent liquidation"*. Such a claim may be brought by a liquidator of the company. Wrongful trading is a civil offence but it is very serious, carrying penalties including disqualification from being a director for 15 years.

If you continue to trade while you have actual knowledge that the company is unable to pay its debts as they become due, then this becomes the extremely serious offence of **fraudulent trading**. This not only carries the disqualification and contribution penalties, but, as it is a criminal offence to carry on trading with this knowledge, there is also the possibility of being imprisoned for up to seven years.

In order to minimise your risk of falling foul of insolvency law, it is essential that you:

- take advice from an insolvency expert if you are unsure about your solvency
- stop trading at once and take advice very quickly if you know you cannot pay your debts as they become due.

These actions will not eliminate your liability, but they will demonstrate that you are doing the best you can and acting with care and skill, which, as detailed above, is a statutory duty and may offer you some mitigation if legal proceedings are issued.

Health and safety

UK company directors have multiple duties to ensure the health, safety and welfare of their employees, customers and anyone else who may be affected by their activities. Strangely, this also includes trespassers on your premises. The Health and Safety at Work Act 1974 states: *"where a company is shown to have committed a health and safety offence, an individual director may also be criminally liable if the corporate offence was committed with their consent or connivance"* (that is, the director was aware of the circumstances but turned a blind eye) or if the offence was attributable to the director's neglect.

Health and safety legislation is some of the most onerous legislation in the UK for directors, and ignorance of it will never be a legally acceptable excuse. *A Health and Safety Guide for Directors* is a highly recommended publication jointly written by the Institute of Directors (IoD) and the Health and Safety Executive – it is aimed specifically at directors and should be a must-read. (See www.healthandsafetyatwork. com.)

The environment

There are many environmental offences that can be committed by a company, particularly in relation to pollution and waste disposal. Where an offence is committed with the directors' consent or connivance, or because of their neglect, they may also be liable.

Bribery Act 2010

This Act makes it a criminal offence for a company to bribe another person, accept a bribe or bribe a foreign public official. *"Directors of a company may also be guilty where the company's offence was committed with their consent or connivance."* As I write, due to the onerous nature of this Act, particularly for smaller companies, it is being rewritten to dilute some of the requirements for these more modest companies.

Pensions Act 2004

This includes provisions that could make a director personally liable for a pension scheme deficit.

Employment law

This is some of the fastest-changing legislation, partly because of its political slant, substantial case law and the opposing positions of the employer and the employee.

In the UK, directors are responsible for numerous employment issues, including:

- maternity and paternity rights
- the minimum wage
- the working time directive
- redundancy rights
- sickness and absenteeism management
- discrimination.

In employment legislation, there is a presumption of guilt on the side of the employer. If a claim is brought against an employer who has selected a man rather than a woman for a particular job, the onus is on the employer to show that the selection was in no way related to gender. If the defence is unsuccessful, the directors of the company could be corporately or personally liable.

ADDITIONAL LEGAL PRINCIPLES

In addition to all these general duties and regulations, there are certain legal principles that directors must adhere to.

As we have seen in the Companies Act 2006, directors of UK companies have a duty to act in the way most likely to promote the success of the company as a whole. Where there is an actual or potential conflict between the interests of the company and the personal interests of a director, you must always give preference to the company

Inter-director and company transactions

You need to be careful how you act if you are buying from or selling to your company. The test for compliance relates to whether the transaction value is the lower of either £100,000 or 10% of the company's net asset value, as shown in a company's latest accounts. The shareholders of the company need to approve the deal if it falls outside these parameters. An example of this could be something as modest as a director buying a car from the business. For example, if the car is £30,000 and the business balance sheet is £200,000, such a transaction would need shareholder approval, as the value of the car is more than 10% of the company's value.

Director loans

Loans involving a company and a director are generally permitted if shareholders have given their approval and if they *"promote the success of the company"*. To some extent, this is a subjective decision on the part of the accountant or auditor, but my advice is that you should always seek professional confirmation.

If the loan is less than £10,000, shareholder approval is not required, nor is it required if the loan is directly for business purposes.

INTERNATIONAL PERSPECTIVES

In our global economy, your ambitions may stretch to international roles in which the law and regulations may be entirely different to those in the UK.

The following is merely an outline of major differences and similarities. It is not a comprehensive list but rather is meant to highlight the need to research such a post thoroughly before accepting it.

United States of America

In the US, only those companies that are publicly limited (i.e. those in which the general public can buy and sell shares) must file accounts that are available to the public. This is not the same as in the UK, where **all** companies, publicly limited or not, must provide accounts.

As in the UK, there is a vast legal framework, with corporate governance practices and directors' duties regulated by both the statutory law of the state in which the corporation is incorporated and federal statutory law.

The US has not adopted a corporate governance code; instead, corporate governance requirements are imposed primarily by various federal laws. However, the listing standards of registered stock exchanges require listed companies to maintain specified corporate governance practices, a requirement that is not unlike our own UK Corporate Governance Code.

A critical difference in the US is the ability to limit the liability of the director much more fully than in the UK, where limitation of liability is very restricted and largely only applies to claims for actions committed prior to appointment. Most states allow a corporation (the name by which a company is generally known in the US) to eliminate or limit directors' personal liability to the corporation or its shareholders for breach of their fiduciary duty. As a result, most corporations adopt provisions in their certificates of incorporation eliminating directors' liability to the fullest extent permitted by law.

Republic of Ireland

An Irish company must have at least one European Economic Area (EEA) resident director. All other standard legislation essentially follows the UK model.

France

The main differences in France relate to gender (see more in Chapter 7) and age restrictions, along with prerequisites for certain companies to have employee representatives on their boards (which is, interestingly, forbidden in Italy and Japan).

In companies with over 50 employees, workers' council representatives sit on the board without voting rights. In the UK, companies with over 50 staff must consult with their staff on matters that affect their strategic well-being but such workers have no right to a board position.

Also, except when otherwise provided for in the by-laws of the region, the number of directors aged over 70 cannot exceed one-third of the total and the age limit for the chair and CEO is 65.

India

A director must be at least 18 years old and an independent director must be at least 21 years old. The minimum age for an MD is 25 years.

There are no nationality restrictions on the appointment of directors, except in certain sectors. For example, companies engaged in the telecommunications sector and the defence sector must have a majority of Indian directors, and companies providing security services (in the private sector) cannot have foreign directors.

HOW TO PROTECT YOURSELF

The legislation relating to being a director may appear onerous, but that doesn't mean it is all going to go horribly wrong. For one thing, you can take measures to minimise the risk, just as you would do in any other situation.

Alongside ongoing and pre-appointment due diligence, and directors' and officers' liability insurance, as discussed earlier in this chapter, here are a few ideas to consider. In all cases, take professional advice.

Transferring assets

It may be possible for a director to transfer personal assets to an entity such as a family trust to provide protection against potential liabilities. Such a decision should be made only after the commercial, legal and taxation implications have been considered. The implications of transferring assets within the family or externally are vast and can impact on future generations. This is a big decision, although it is not uncommon in very wealthy families, so specialist advice is essential.

The more you know, the better you will be protected

Ask questions and be seen to ask questions, and don't be fobbed off with non-answers. If you don't understand, keep asking until you do.

Keep your own record of meeting notes and board minutes. These personal notes are very persuasive evidence if you need them as they are difficult to replicate.

If you are concerned about anything, always seek professional advice. In listed companies, under the UK Corporate Governance Code such advice must be paid for by the company. If you are a director of an unlisted company, you may have to pay for this advice yourself, but it will be money well spent if you have grave concerns about something.

If all this scares the life out of you, it may be possible for the company to indemnify a director against liabilities under certain very limited circumstances. However, it cannot exempt a director from liability to the company for breach of duty, negligence, criminal activity or any other default. Any attempt to do so would be void.

Good practice guidelines

In terms of self-preservation, nothing works better than basic sensible and practical measures.

If, for example, you can demonstrate to a court that throughout your directorship you have done all you can to comply with the multiple statutory rule books and have been at pains to act properly, you will have the makings of a good case for mitigation.

PLCs on the London stock exchange must comply with the **UK Corporate Governance Code**; if they don't, they have to state why not. Although the Code is not law, and it does not apply to unlisted companies, as a code of good practice it is well worth looking at, if only to investigate ideal behaviour.

The Code is regarded as exemplary practice for boards and companies and covers the following headings:

- leadership
- effectiveness
- accountability
- remuneration
- relations with shareholders.

It also provides guidelines on the following:

- the board
- the chair
- non-executive directors
- remuneration
- risk and accountability
- shareholders.

You can download the UK Corporate Governance Code at www.frc. org.uk/Our-Work/Codes-Standards/Corporate-governance/UK-Corporate-Governance-Code.aspx.

The IoD has also created a code for unlisted companies, which is available at www.iod.com. Again, this is a code and not law, but, like the UK Corporate Governance Code, it sets out good practice and, if followed, would provide evidence of acting with care and skill.

IN SUMMARY

As one judge famously said: *"Act with sunshine."* Be honest and open in all you do. Transparency is the key to maximising your protection. Keep minutes and personal records and ensure that you have the right to retain these after your role has ended (to defend yourself later, if necessary). Nothing is completely safe, but following a few simple guidelines and always asking for clarification will help.

Chapter 3

Getting the job

"The secret of success is to know something nobody else knows."
Aristotle Onassis

The following chapter considers the next and very important part of your route to the boardroom – getting the job in the first place. It will show you how to make yourself aware of available opportunities, and how to make the right first impression at interview.

Even in the twenty-first century, who you know, and who knows you, is an important factor in success in corporate life. There are still some companies, and arguably some entire professions, where the right name and the right school tie count as much as any qualifications or relevant experience you may have.

But it is also entirely possible to get noticed for the right reasons, and without an advantageous background. It is just something you will need to work at.

MY OWN EXPERIENCE

My dream was always to be a board director, even when I wasn't quite sure what it was! I'm not sure if I was attracted to the wooden 12-foot board table or the impressive lunches that were wheeled in across the finance department, or whether I just wanted a seat at the table where decisions affecting my future were made. Whatever it was, I had focus and determination and still do.

I am fortunate in that I cannot recall many examples of direct discrimination, but I did have a constant personal need to prove I was worthy of the post. In hindsight, this was almost certainly due to a lack of confidence rather than any physical or psychological issue. I do recognise that this is not always the case, and perhaps I was just blissfully unaware, but either way I was always fiercely focused on the end goal.

GETTING NOTICED

It is all very well being a good all-rounder, but the few things you do better than anyone else are what really matter. You have to stand out and find the one thing that you are better at than your peers. This could be networking, public speaking or blogging. Whatever it is, identify it and make sure that others notice it as soon as it becomes relevant.

Know your goals and objectives

If you don't know or understand what your destination is, then you are likely to be perceived as unfocused. This isn't acceptable for directors. Your short-term objectives may change over time, but you should have, and be seen to have, clear long-term goals for both yourself and the companies you work for.

In your day-to-day life, knowing that you want to travel overseas, for instance, is a good start, but you will probably be able to plan better if you know which country you want to go to – and better still if you know which city.

Think of your career as a road map to your final destination. You may well go off course from time to time, but at least make sure that your personal satnav is aiming for a precise destination.

Play to your strengths

None of us is good at everything. I know my weaknesses, although I don't necessarily like to admit to them openly, but I also know what I am good at. In my case, I can deal with problems head-on. I am very well connected and can see through the issues and get straight to the point. I also think I am very fair and straight-talking. I like to share my successes and am not afraid of making mistakes. Although these personality traits are not unique, my particular mixture of them is unique (and so will yours be!).

I didn't come from a wealthy family. I don't have a blue-blooded education, I lost my mother when I was 16, and shortly afterwards my father's business went bust, leaving us temporarily homeless. I don't offer this as a sob story, but these are events that have shaped my personality. They have made me strong, determined, focused and sometimes very insecure, which by implication has made me something of a workaholic.

Nurture your professional relationships

Build your database of contacts from the first moment you can in your career — or even before you start your career. If you help people out when they need assistance, then people will help you out too. Giving back is the best way of getting on. This can help build your reputation and help you make important friendships.

Take the time to build and nurture relationships with everyone. Don't discard anyone — that way you will establish a network of "allies". I have thousands of contacts on my iPhone, including some I haven't heard from for years, but I know that many of them would be there for me if I needed them.

Also, develop your network outside office hours. Socialising with colleagues after work often makes everyone feel more relaxed and open to new friendships.

I was given a great tip by someone who had had some of the best sales training available from Proctor & Gamble. He said that after any appointment or meeting, he would go back to his car and jot down any personal details about the client, such as the age of their children or where they went on holiday. This meant that the next time he met the customer he could refer to the card, and that made the person feel very special. It is such an easy process, and now with the advent of business card readers on smart phones it can take only seconds to process and then access information.

Never lose a contact, and try to get in touch with the less active members of your network from time to time. One lady I know used to go through her iPhone contacts at random on long journeys and send a "not heard from you for ages – how are things?" email to anyone who had been quiet for a while.

We are all a bit "spammed out", so don't send useless information around the internet. Well placed comments and suggestions are always welcome, however.

I have found that people have asked me to join their board not just because of my contacts and knowledge, but because they liked me!

So make sure you are personable, contactable, appreciative, friendly, willing and above all amenable.

Shout about your achievements

Keep track of all of your achievements. If clients or colleagues pay you a compliment, write it down. If the compliment comes in an email, print it out and keep it.

Sadly, women in particular are often not immediately receptive to a positive statement (we have all at some point said: "What, this old thing?!"). It is important not only to give well deserved praise, but to know when to accept it graciously.

Bite the bullet

Unfortunately, when you are rising through the ranks, some people can become jealous and sometimes even vindictive. This can take the form of stealing your ideas and presenting them as their own, or blatantly taking credit for tasks you have carried out successfully.

You have two courses of action if this happens. One is to put it down to experience and learn from the process. The other is to make a point of publicly pointing out the "misunderstanding", but if you choose this route, be prepared for the consequences.

As I have grown older, greyer and wiser, the latter option has always been my chosen course, but on the way to the top I have not always been so confident and have recognised the political implications of "outing" an offender, particularly when this has been a person senior to me.

Take every opportunity you can

Be the first to put your hand up to volunteer, especially for the tasks no one else wants. This will get you noticed and that is what is important – but do make sure you always deliver.

Get out and about

I really don't like networking – to be honest, not many people do. But without serious efforts on your part in this area, you are less likely to succeed. So go to the staff functions and the industry events and be seen as a player. The cost to you is your time, but it is time well spent – most ambitious people like to work with people they have met and those who have been recommended by people they know.

Be nice to people!

This is one of the most important values to me. It is so easy to be friendly and kind and I am always amazed that not everyone behaves in this way. Being nice can help you deal with very difficult people and situations and, when used correctly and in a genuine manner, it can be very disarming.

Keep abreast of the market

Google, LinkedIn and the like provide a vast array of information, so there is no excuse not to be aware of industry trends. Where relevant, create your own news stories; the more you know, the more creative you can be with ideas and suggestions.

Find a mentor

Probably the most important person in your career progression is your mentor, that individual you can talk to, share ideas with, cry with and moan to. This person will not be your friend but they will be the person you turn to for support throughout your career. I have had a number of mentors throughout my life and I could not have managed certain issues without their honesty and frankness. Choose wisely. They do not always need payment but, on the other hand, it *is* a job and you need to feel you can call this person when you need them, so paying them sometimes satisfies that guilt.

Use personal PR

Until you become famous, you won't have the luxury of having a personal publicist, but you shouldn't need one anyway. In 25 years in business, I have rarely used a professional PR firm, yet I am widely known in my field. This hasn't happened by accident: I work very hard at it and I have made excellent contacts with the press and journalists over the years, often by providing them with storylines that are regularly in demand be it an award win, a new contract or a new local employment or apprentice scheme initiative. It doesn't really matter; just make it relevant to the media you are connecting with.

I have always been happy to speak on the radio, and more recently on television, and I enter multiple awards, including Business Woman of the Year and Non-executive Director of the Year. Of course, I don't win them all, nor would I expect to, but being nominated does increase your media profile.

Watch your social media

Whatever your personal opinion about how Facebook, LinkedIn groups or Twitter connections should work or how the world should be, social media are public forums. It has taken me some time, as a woman of a certain age, to embrace social media. Indeed, I started using Twitter only in the last six months, but now I am a frequent user and love the opportunity to share thoughts and ideas with my followers.

However, you need to be very careful about your social media profile, as cyberspace lasts forever and inappropriate behaviour will be noted even if it was something you did in your own time.

Dress to impress

Business attire is much less formal than it was 20 years ago even in the professions, once the bastion of suits and ties, but my advice is to go very carefully down the casual dress route. Be guided by what your colleagues are wearing, but – especially in the early days of a new appointment – it is wise to err on the side of caution.

Dressing well doesn't mean dressing expensively – there are plenty of high street retailers with great bargains – but it does mean dressing discreetly. Ostentatious jewellery and a heavy dose of scent can give the wrong first impression, and that can be difficult to overcome.

MY OWN EXPERIENCE

Although I may appear to ooze self-confidence, in fact it's a bit of a charade. Like many people I have numerous doubts and uncertainties – I have just got better over the years at hiding them. My personal method was always to be very well groomed, wearing the best clothes I could afford. I always wore something a bit different but not *too* different. Most importantly, I always chose something that gave me confidence. This has enabled me to deal with difficult, challenging and scary occasions.

Shout about it again!

It is not a sin to be successful. If you don't want to be overlooked, you must let people know what you can do. Done sensitively, this is not boasting – it is positive self-publicity. Don't be afraid to say you are not at all bad, or even great, at what you do.

HOW TO RECOGNISE AN OPPORTUNITY FOR A BOARD POSITION

MY OWN EXPERIENCE

It is a recognised truth that you are more likely to regret the things you don't do rather than the things you do.

I have made countless mistakes but I have also had numerous successful moments. On the negative side, I didn't buy the most suitable business property I was offered as it was, in my opinion at the time, overpriced. Twenty years on, and with the benefit of hindsight, I can see it would have been a fabulous investment. I have recruited certain people who have spun me a line, even giving them shares in my business, only to be severely disappointed by their lack of enthusiasm and disappointing work ethic.

On the positive side, I have also invested in so-called no-hopers who expressed a wish to improve themselves, and have been fabulously proud of their achievements. I have started businesses without too much thought, planning or even money, only to be astounded by their success, which has appeared almost by chance.

I'd like my tombstone to read: *"She gave it her best shot."*

What does *your* opportunity look like?

Some people don't seem to be able to recognise opportunities. Perhaps they are not looking or they are looking the wrong way, or perhaps it looks a bit too much like hard work or is somehow overly complicated.

A good friend of mine started a virtual personal assistant (PA) service to provide high-quality secretarial support and other PA-type services, from picking up the dry cleaning and choosing birthday presents to booking flights. The service was aimed at busy executives who needed this help but not all the time, so their requirements didn't warrant a full-time PA.

At a girly lunch one day we were all discussing how marvellous this idea was and wasn't it great that our friend was doing so well, when one of the ladies present said: *"Well, I suggested this to her a couple of years ago but it just wasn't the right time and now she has taken my idea and is making a great success of it."*

No idea or opportunity is truly original, but turning a concept into reality is what is important. Saying you were going to do it just doesn't count!

Don't be afraid to use your contacts

Your contacts are a great source of advice and information, but if you use them you should always pay them back double with any help you can provide to them. This isn't just good manners – you can benefit too. I have found that the more I help without expecting anything in return, the more I get back.

MY OWN EXPERIENCE

Two years ago I started an apprenticeship scheme in my business. This has been one of the best things I have ever done by far; I feel so privileged to have taken these young people who have previously struggled to achieve, and to have helped them get on the right path. I started the scheme because I wanted to give something back to my community, but in fact the rewards have all been mine. I now have wonderfully inspired young people working for me who are tremendously loyal and have a great work ethic. They have improved my business immensely.

I first heard about this scheme through one of the clients on whose board I sit. They provided me with the relevant contacts and I have never looked back. Throughout your life, a few great opportunities will land on your doorstep, but whether or not you recognise or act upon them is up to you.

Opportunities won't always be perfect

Very little is, and in my experience things sometimes go wrong long before they start to go right. Certainly, in my case, for every one success there have been 99 failures. The secret is to just keep moving forward. Put the negatives behind you and seek out the positives.

MY OWN EXPERIENCE

I started my career as a bookkeeper in an owner-managed business working for an ambitious man. Within three years I was finance director and company secretary. I was an accounting professional, so bookkeeper had seemed a lowly post, but I could see that I could add value very quickly and that the owner would, and did, reward success.

Find your inspiration

For me it was my mother. She had inherited her father's sheet metal engineering business at 20 years of age. In the 1960s it was unthinkable that a woman would be a sheet metal worker, let alone the MD and a shareholder, but until, sadly, she died prematurely of breast cancer at 50, she ran a successful business in an extremely male-dominated world. I have always thought that if she could succeed in such trying circumstances, then anyone can. Identify your "Inspirer". It could be a famous successful person like Richard Branson, it could be a story you heard in the news or one told in the local pub, but find someone who you can align your own particular star with and go for it.

Don't be afraid, or learn to hide it

I speak at over 80 events every year, often in front of an audience of the great and the good, of highly intelligent and well informed people, and I am always wracked with nerves as I go up to the podium. However often I speak in public, the nerves don't go away. I have been told that this is a good thing as it keeps you on your toes and stops you becoming overly confident – though these platitudes are no use at all when you're actually there! I have learned to deal with my nerves by going to the ladies just before my speech and giving myself a pep talk: *"You can do this! What's the worst that could happen?"* And, of course, once I am on stage everything invariably goes well. But getting there is always a challenge.

Dressing the part helps me. If I feel physically good about myself, somehow I have more confidence. Do whatever you need to do to stand up to the job. But if you don't feel you can, you are in good company – Dame Judi Dench has admitted to crucifying nerves before every performance.

Put people first

> # MY OWN EXPERIENCE
>
> I have bad moods and occasionally Winston Churchill's "black dog" engulfs me. What I don't do is bring it to the office. I have a low staff turnover and I believe my staff and clients alike enjoy working for and with me.
>
> I always try to treat them how I would like to be treated. I don't always succeed – business pressures can sometimes be overwhelming – but I do everything I can to be kind and genuine.

Work at building relationships with people and opportunities will follow. Everything is about relationships and relationships are about give and take. Always be kind and charming. People remember that, and, frankly, it is so much easier than being nasty!

Once you start the process of personal development and begin to take up opportunities that could result in interviews, it is of course very important to make every encounter count!

THE INTERVIEW

All this hard work, determination and stamina will be to no avail if you can't get past the first interview. This may be formal or informal, a chat over coffee, an early evening drink or a formal panel of seemingly scary and officious current board members – find out which it is beforehand.

Here are some important tips to make sure you maximise the opportunity. Of course, many of these apply to any interview process, be it for a more junior role or for your dream directorship.

It isn't a myth that appointment decisions, particularly negative ones, can be made within a few moments of meeting, but it *is* a myth that you cannot turn around negative perceptions, as long as you are aware of them. Body language, tone of voice and just being enthusiastic are all as important as what you actually say. Don't be arrogant or stuffy or pretentious. Be honest and open and be seen to be questioning and creative, whatever the post.

Tips for a successful interview

Don't wing it
Know the company and know what you can bring to the business. There is simply no excuse for ignorance, as there is an overwhelming amount of information in the public domain. If you come to my company for an interview and have not bothered to find out anything about me, I will think that you are rude and uninterested.

Dress appropriately
Make sure that what you wear matches the company culture and is appropriate for the role you want. Many companies now have a "corporate casual" style, but check with your contacts to see what they require. When in doubt, always err on the side of formal business attire. There is also a bit of a north–south divide where dress is concerned – northern-based businesses tend to be more formal.

Arrive early
Whether you are coming by car, train or bus, you need to give yourself plenty of time. Delays happen, often for reasons beyond your control, but what you can do is anticipate this. It is much better to sit in the local coffee shop gathering your thoughts than rush in late and bedraggled for a critical interview.

Show enthusiasm and spirit
Following many recruitment disasters, I now always recruit on enthusiasm. It is hard to fake and difficult to create, whereas skills I can train. If you don't *really* want to work for me, I am not sure I want you in my team.

Be self-confident and friendly
Self-confidence is not the same as arrogance, and being friendly is not the same as being overly familiar. If you can demonstrate real confidence and self-worth and still be friendly, then it is likely an interviewer will warm to you quickly.

Have some questions ready

You know the one: "So is there anything you would like to ask us?" The answer is always yes! Have some relevant, interesting questions prepared. Here are a couple of good ones that I have used in the past.

- How soon can I add value?
- What is the most critical issue facing the business and the board at the moment?

Be animated

I have known some interviewees drift off into their own world. Now this could, of course, be because of my interviewing style, but it is not acceptable to sit and nod; you must remain involved and ask questions for clarification, but be wary of interrupting your interviewer too much.

Bring your CV to life

If the interviewer has had a whole day of panel interviews and you are in the last group, they may be feeling a little jaded, so discuss the benefits you will bring to the business.

I really appreciate it when someone gives me real examples of how they have dealt with particular issues by putting things into context and telling a story. I am more engaged and far more responsive.

Don't be afraid to discuss the things that haven't gone quite right, but equally don't hold back on your achievements. As I have said before, it is generally not a good idea to hide your light under a bushel if you want to succeed in the corporate world, and an interview is definitely not the place for false modesty. Shout about your successes!

Answer concisely

Rambling responses show a lack of clarity and even a lack of confidence. Answer the question asked, not the one you hoped would be asked. You can always provide additional information at a later stage. Where possible, give real-life examples of when you have applied a particular behaviour.

Don't forget your closing remarks

No sale is complete until you close it. Unless you have firmly decided during the course of the interview that the post holds no appeal, you should clearly state your ongoing interest. Don't go overboard – this is not the time for gushing statements – but leave the interviewer or panel in no doubt about your enthusiasm. (On the other hand, if you have decided that this role is not for you, it is also a courtesy to the interviewer to let them know.)

The interview questions

Over the course of my career, I have interviewed scores of people and without a doubt it is just as tortuous a process for the interviewer as it is for the interviewee. Most first interviews for a board role last between one and two hours – much less and it is likely you were not viewed favourably; much more and you both may start to lose the will to progress.

Second interviews, and there are often as many as four or five interviews for a senior board position, can take much longer and may involve off-site visits. But you won't have a chance of getting to that second interview if you blow it at the first one.

If this is a non-executive director role, it is possible you haven't had an interview of any kind for many years. Do not assume you know what it will feel like.

Although the approach could vary slightly depending on whether you are applying for an internal promotion or an external opportunity, there are some standard questions you should come prepared for at the interview.

Tell me about yourself

I have yet to attend any sort of interview where this isn't asked directly or indirectly. The interviewer does not want to know about your GCSE passes or your first Saturday job, so keep it brief and light.

Have you any experience in this field?

Talk about specifics that relate to the board to which you are applying. If you do not have direct experience, get as close as you can for executive jobs. For many non-executive director roles, industry experience is largely irrelevant – not having specific experience means that you can stay out of operational areas – but not all interviewers will agree with this view so try to gauge the situation as you progress.

Is success important to you?

The answer has to be yes, but be clear that you don't value success at the expense of others or things you hold dear, whatever these may be. This can seem like a trick question, but it isn't; it is a way of assessing your personality and enthusiasm.

Would you say you are popular?

There is a lovely song from the stage show *Wicked* that implies that people are successful because they are popular. However, being a director isn't a popularity contest. Although it is important in corporate life to be liked and respected, popularity is by no means essential for business success.

Be prepared to talk about how you have had to deal with issues in ways that have certainly not made you popular, but that the outcomes have been positive. Where possible, give examples to demonstrate this.

Are you applying for other jobs?

Be honest, but do not spend a lot of time on this area. Keep the focus on *this* role and what you can do for *this* company.

Why do you want to join this company board?

Sincerity is extremely important here and will be sensed by the interviewer. Relate the role to your long-term career goals.

Do you know anyone else who works for us?

This could be an issue, as some companies have policies that forbid relatives from working together, for instance. However, if you do have a contact at any level in the company, you must clearly let the interviewer know.

Do you have a salary in mind?

Of course you do, and at some point this will need a full and frank discussion. However, the first interview is probably not the best time for this. Either you can try to defer a detailed discussion to a later conversation, or you can gently bat the question back and ask the interviewer what she has in mind.

Have you ever been asked to leave a board?

If you haven't, then say no, clearly and unambiguously. If you have, be honest and brief, and avoid saying negative things about the people or company involved.

Explain how you would be an asset to this board

Highlight your best points as they relate to the position being discussed.

Why should we hire you?

Point out the ways in which your assets meet the company's needs. Do not mention any other candidates to make a comparison.

What irritates you about fellow board members?

Be honest but brief.

What is your greatest strength?

Stay positive. You could talk about your ability to prioritise, your problem-solving skills, your ability to work under pressure, your professional expertise, your leadership skills, your positive attitude, or even your black book of contacts.

What would your previous board or employer say your strongest point is?

If you are astute, you will have come armed with glowing references. If not, avoid bland answers. Think of something positive that is a little bit different – perhaps you are imaginative, or a problem-solver, or particularly tenacious.

Tell me about the worst board you have worked with

This is a genuine question I have been asked before. As tempting as it might be to vent your frustrations – don't! Stick to generalities.

NEARLY THERE!

Persistence is a virtue in my opinion. You cannot give up, however many times you are rejected. Stamina and determination nearly always win through (providing you have the requisite skills, of course) but you may not be able to start your directorship in a blue-chip PLC.

Sitting on a board is neither as simple nor as difficult as people may think. It isn't true that there is a shortage of directors willing to serve; in fact, it isn't easy to get on a board today. Directors already in post may be becoming more selective about the board invitations they accept, and some highly qualified executives refuse to consider serving at all, but landing your first board seat is still no easy matter.

If you want to become a director, headhunters are generally useless. Such firms are retained to find directors to serve on boards, and not to find board seats for potential directors.

So what can you do?

Unpaid volunteer boards

Serving on a not-for-profit board may help you get onto a commercial board but it isn't a guaranteed rite of passage. If you find out about an opportunity and you meet the initial criteria, the question still remains: how should you go about getting on the board? Some of the steps we have explored apply equally to volunteer or commercial boards, but do not mistake a volunteer position for an easy ride. Considerable time commitment is often required and although unpaid there is often no shortage of candidates who have a personal passion to work in a particular field. You need to impress and show dedication along with availability and commitment. These boards don't want you to practise your skills on them, they need a real job doing.

Smaller or international companies

You are unlikely to get a call from a FTSE 100 company offering you your first board position. In fact, the chances of a position like that ever opening up for most of us are slim. But it is possible that some international companies may be interested in having individuals who have UK business experience on their boards.

The Lord Davies report on increasing the number of women on FTSE boards is all well and good, but there are far more opportunities to "cut your teeth" and learn the skills of a great director a little further down the corporate tree, so try smaller companies as well.

Investigate these types of companies and be proactive. Contact them and ask for a meeting. Most will say no, but one may just say yes. You have nothing to lose but the time and effort needed to make an approach. Getting that first board seat remains a challenge, even for highly qualified business leaders. But once you land your first, more board invitations will follow.

Chapter 4

What makes a good board?

"The difficult I'll do right now. The
impossible will take a little while."
from 'Crazy He Calls Me' (1949), by
Carl Sigman and Bob Russell

Asking what makes a good director is a bit like asking what makes a good mother or father. It depends on the age of the children, on the issue in hand, on how the individual is feeling that day, and on what other pressures they are facing. No two people parent in exactly the same way. Is good parenting signified by a happy child, a calm teenager or a successful graduate? I would suggest that this is far too simplistic and likely to be wholly inaccurate. In my experience, siblings brought up in the same household by the same parents in the same manner often turn out to be total opposites.

This chapter will look at both positive and negative personality traits for a potential director. It will also explore some of the mistakes directors have made, some of them now infamous. It will examine best practice for a board meeting and, finally, give you some practical tools to assist you in your day-to-day performance.

MY OWN EXPERIENCE

My craft has been honed over many posts, both executive and non-executive, and is not just due to academic qualifications. Mirroring good practice and avoiding the bad are essential traits. Watch, listen and learn.

One of my first chairs made a special effort between meetings to personally contact each of the other directors. This was done in the guise of a cosy chat, but in hindsight was all about gaining our confidence.

One of the most charismatic CEOs I worked for encouraged and arranged for regular director development – this was at a time when this wasn't at all common. The result was an engaged and loyal board who felt confident to challenge and support the CEO.

On the negative side, I have witnessed divisive practices, such as the scary finance director who produced what could only be fictitious numbers in order to sway the rest of the board from a common objective.

THE PERSONALITY TRAITS OF A DIRECTOR

A good director will likely be made rather than born – and made by experience rather than anything else. I have been on numerous training courses and have read countless books, but my skills have been honed in post and on the route to the boardroom. And I have learned as much from poor directors as from those inspirational people I have been privileged to watch in action. At every board meeting I attend (as many as six a month), I always learn something new, particularly about human behaviour. These are the insights that I hope to share.

Watch, listen and learn

It is impossible to overestimate the importance of listening. When you reach your ultimate goal and are sitting comfortably in the boardroom, at times it is difficult to hear what others are saying. This is not because you are temporarily deaf, but because when we believe we have something very important to impart there is a tendency to stop listening to others. This is made worse if you do not agree with your colleagues' comments. If you are planning your retort before your fellow director has finished speaking, you are probably not alone, but the problem is that you haven't heard the full story and, as a result, your reply may well be inadequate. We all have off days for varying reasons, but there are some positive traits that a great director should work on.

The positive traits

- Look at the big picture – operational details are not the responsibility of the board. Don't get bogged down in the detail and don't interfere with management. Your job is to support them; it isn't to do their job. Prioritise, prioritise, prioritise. It is a big and complex job directing the interests of a business. You cannot deal with everything but you will have to learn what must be dealt with first.
- Reflect, then act; not the other way round. Shooting from the hip is not the role of a director. On the other hand, neither is constant procrastination.
- Look after your people – *all* of them. Make them feel valued and appreciated. Ensure that proper appraisals and good reward systems are in place and treat everyone as an equal. After all, honey attracts many more flies than vinegar.
- Can you give an elevator speech about your vision and mission? Do you live by your corporate values? A great director lives and breathes them. Can you visualise your destination, touch it, smell it?

Some sources of inspiration

- Richard Reed, Adam Balon and Jon Wright, the founders of Innocent Drinks, have a company mantra that reads: *"We want to leave things better than we found them."* They practise what they preach, giving 10% of all profits to the Innocent Foundation.

- John Bird, *The Big Issue* founder, is on a mission to eradicate the plight of the homeless. John had been a homeless teenager himself but has been very successful, now turning over £6.5m p.a. and investing in 150 UK businesses.
- James Dyson, founder of the eponymous company, refused to give up on his ideas, despite years and years of rejections. He now has a net worth of $4.2 billion.
- Finally, it wouldn't be possible to look at high-performing directors without mentioning Virgin founder Sir Richard Branson. Even though he has had numerous less successful ventures, which have cost him billions, he regards them as excellent mistakes. He has been quoted as saying: *"My interests in life come from setting huge, apparently unbelievable, challenges and trying to rise above them."*

The negative traits

Of course, for every good trait there are numerous negative ones that unfortunately too many directors embrace.

Interfering with management

Leave them to it. Provide personal support but don't interfere at an operational level.

Personally, I have done this many times, partly because of my difficulty with delegation – I just can't delegate as much as I should, and some might even call me a control freak! However, the fact is that if you want to grow the business, you must be able to rise above the day-to-day running of it and trust management to look after this.

Inadequate support

Although the board isn't necessarily a team, unlike a management team, a good director must know when to support her fellow board members. If your role is finance, don't leave your fellow directors behind by using financial jargon. Don't forget that the board is only as good as its weakest link. If you sense a lack of understanding, then take the time to support those who need help. It could well be that you will need some help in the future.

However, if you don't like the way your fellow directors are running the business, you should say so and insist on your views being minuted. But choose your moment, and your words, carefully. Being destructive is not helpful; use a constructive approach first. If your concerns become more serious, seek legal advice at the earliest possible stage.

Making business gaffes

Ryanair boss Michael O'Leary called thousands of his passengers *"idiots"* in a furious rant. He said that customers who turned up at the airport without a printed boarding pass were *"stupid"*.

Gerald Ratner said: *"We also do cut-glass sherry decanters complete with six glasses on a silver-plated tray that your butler can serve you drinks on, all for £45.95. People say, 'How can you sell this for such a low price?' I say, because it's total crap."* His confession led to him being thrown off the board as sales collapsed before the chain was renamed.

Virgin boss Sir Richard Branson once told a journalist: *"Do you know why we are changing the name of Virgin trains? Because they are f****d."*

Chief executive of lottery operator Camelot, Dianne Thompson, blundered when she said that players have virtually no chance of scooping the jackpot and would be lucky enough to win a tenner.

Watch what you say in public. At best, gaffes like this are unwelcome for the company; at worst, you could find yourself held up to public ridicule and quoted in books like this for years to come ...

Failing to ask questions

There is no such thing as a stupid question. Ask them all without fear. It is your job to ask for clarification. A great question for a non-executive director is: "What's the critical issue we are facing today?"

Taking too many risks

It is not only a legal requirement but it makes business sense to manage risk. Risk has both positive and negative implications and an astute director will recognise the opportunities as well as the downsides.

HOW TO HAVE A GREAT BOARD MEETING

Although decisions are made on an ongoing basis by individual directors, running the strategic direction of the business starts in the boardroom. In order to be a dynamic and efficient director, it is important that you function within properly formatted board meetings. These will undoubtedly improve your skills and the company's performance. If no framework exists for meetings, make it your responsibility to introduce one.

There are multiple ways of improving a board meeting, or indeed any meeting, and the suggestions below apply to both large and small organisations and to voluntary bodies, from school boards to charities.

Who should sit around the table

Just as we are not able to choose our ideal football team, we are rarely able to choose our ideal board. However, if you could, these would be my suggestions. As well as the senior independent non-executive director, several other posts could also be non-executive. For example, the chair is often a non-executive post. The board of an SME may only have one non-executive director, but the larger the business the more NEDs you are likely to find around the table. The UK Corporate Governance Code states that for every executive you should have a corresponding NED, excluding the chair.

The ideal board should contain five to seven members. Odd numbers work because it prevents deadlock, and these numbers are sufficient for a good debate but not so many that nothing can be achieved.

MY OWN EXPERIENCE

One of the more challenging boards I ever sat on had 32 members!

Clearly the problem with this number is that it's just too large to have a sensible debate. What happened in practice in this board, which was mostly a voluntary group of people, was that decisions were more easily made in the various board committees. This isn't effective governance and tended to create an "us and them" culture.

So, smaller numbers work better, but they should not be so small that they prevent sufficient dialogue and debate.

Here are some individuals who might make up the ideal five- or seven-person board.

- **The sales person:** As head of sales, this person needs to understand the market, the customers and where the next new idea is coming from. They need a persuasive and engaging personality. They also need to be mentally robust as this role requires more than average stamina and determination.
- **The IT expert:** I can hardly think of a business where IT understanding is not vital. The problem is that most board members have little or no substantial IT skills, so this individual needs to be able to discuss technology issues in a language the board can relate to.
- **The CEO or MD:** As a leader of the business and an interface between the board and the management team, this person needs to be a strategic thinker and have great implementation skills in addition to being a good delegator. They must engender respect and ensure that the board strategy is carried out.
- **The chair:** This person must have great listening skills but at the same time be decisive. They must be a leader and be inclusive. They must also have the skills to know when to leave the rest of the board to make things happen.
- **Senior independent non-executive director:** The conscience of the board, well connected and well regarded, this person supports the chair and often deputises for her. Ideally they should have no material interests in the business to allow for as much impartiality as possible.
- **The operations director:** This is the person who gets things done and is often in the thick of it when logistical problems arise. Practical, down-to-earth and no-nonsense, this role is about seeing a problem through to its solution, before it becomes a crisis.
- **The ideas person:** This is the individual who will always come up with a creative solution. They always manage to

find a way round an issue and to take a crisis and turn it into an opportunity.

- **The numbers person:** This person needs to have a clear head and strong independent personality. They need to deliver difficult and often negative news in a clear, coherent manner.

Collectively, a board should provide guidance, support and connections.

Some practical tips to make board meetings run smoothly

Start in the morning

Mornings are always best for meetings of any sort. People are more alert and energised. Have a "no mobile or smartphone" rule before the meeting and definitely during it. The motto should be: "When you are in the room, you are in the room."

I don't have board meetings on a Monday or a Friday either, as these are usually busier days, so it is more difficult for people to be fully engaged. Also, if you have non-executive directors who have to travel, it is usually easier to travel to and from meetings mid-week.

I also like to have my meetings off-site at least a couple of times a year. This makes them more informal and, as a result, often more productive. Where a client has multiple sites, I also like to make sure we rotate the meetings around the different locations, as it is helpful for the non-executive directors to see the different sites and it makes the board seem less remote to those staff based outside the head office.

Start with conformance matters

In Appendix 3 there is a sample board meeting agenda. Most board meetings require the routine approval of administrative things such as the minutes of the previous meeting and legal formalities. This is called conformance, and once you have got these matters out of the way the majority of the time can be spent on performance. Think of it in the following way: conformance is about the things you should do; performance is about the things you *must* do to drive the business forward.

Be straight talking and honest

Over the years I have sat in many board meetings where far too much of the discussion has been about what happened and what should have happened instead of what the board is going to do to make sure it never happens again. Of course, it helps if you have up-to-date and easily understandable information. Frankly, there is little point in discussing data that is months out of date. Board members also need to be open about their understanding of issues.

Let the chair do their job

The job of the chair is to control the meeting and facilitate cohesive and well thought-out decisions. The chair should not allow board members to use the board meeting as a platform for self-promotion, nor should she allow the meeting to degenerate into a public lynching for any offences committed.

Good meeting manners

All board members should, as a matter of course:

- arrive on time
- read the board papers in advance
- contribute on all matters on the agenda, but not seek to dominate the meeting
- listen properly to everything that is said.

Present solutions

If there is bad news, don't just hide it in a board paper and hope for the best. You should take the time to talk to your fellow board members about it, and, more importantly, as a good director you should arrive at the board meeting with a possible solution, not just the problem. No one has an answer for everything and we all need help and advice from time to time, so you should never be afraid to ask for assistance. However, you are now in a very senior role and therefore you will be expected to offer ideas, and for these ideas to have been properly thought through (and, where appropriate, costed). Solicit feedback to your ideas and don't be too afraid or too proud to make changes as a result of the feedback.

Minutes and your own notes

In preparation for the board meeting, you should always get a copy of the meeting agenda in advance. This will help you to keep up with the flow of the meeting. For meetings held via conference call, the chair should ask everyone to identify themselves by first and last name before contributing to the discussion.

Board minutes should list those present and those contributing remotely (by Skype or conference call), record any apologies for absence and state whether or not the meeting has a proper quorum for decision-making. The minutes should also record the date and location of the meeting.

Good board minutes should reflect the decisions made, who is responsible for actioning them, and the time frame in which they must be implemented. Minutes do not need to detail what everyone said, unless a very serious situation is being dealt with, such as any potential for insolvent trading. In that case I would recommend insisting on verbatim minutes.

As well as formal minutes I have always used a "day book"; in my case this is a diary where I record anything from the meeting that I think is relevant. I don't use this book just for board meetings; I use it for all meetings and have found it very valuable and easy to refer back to when a particular issue is being debated again or even challenged.

Board papers

Appendix 4 at the end of the book contains samples of board papers for both regular issues and specific requirements. The key with all board papers is to keep them clear and concise and avoid technical jargon (this is particularly important where you have non-executive directors from outside the company's sector). The concise format is one that I have developed over many years; I have found it to be very effective and much more likely to be read than many of the lengthy tomes I have received all too regularly.

The board calendar

A board calendar isn't just a list of meeting dates. It should provide for specific items to be discussed on particular dates throughout the year, for example the annual budget, the remuneration report and succession planning. It should be published and agreed annually to allow board members time to plan critical business functions, such as attendance at exhibitions and conferences, around the dates and also to ensure that personal commitments such as holidays do not conflict.

In the meeting

Keeping the meeting focused is the role of the chair, but all members of the board must support this. A board meeting is not the place to discuss details and dissect every item, nor is it the place to score points or to rant and rave or pull apart the management team. It is an opportunity to make strategic decisions and ensure that the management team is on track and has the right resources to achieve the board's objectives.

- A well-managed board meeting should start and finish on time; failure to do so is just plain lazy. Executive and non-executive directors alike are hugely busy. One tip is to assign a certain amount of time to each issue; another is to do a rough calculation of everyone's hourly rate. It is very informative at the end of a meeting to add up these hours and calculate what it has cost you in pounds sterling.
- The agenda should be distributed to board members with sufficient time to allow participants to read it, to respond if necessary, and to request that certain items are included. Ideally this should be at least five working days before the meeting.
- Everyone should read the meeting agenda and board papers thoroughly prior to the meeting. Don't come to the meeting without having read the papers. This is not only very inefficient, it is also rude. However, board papers can be tedious if they are not written properly. Try using my simple templates in Appendix 4 and use a colour-coding system, i.e. a red marker on the top of the report means it *must* be read, whereas a green marker means that it contains additional information or is something the board members may like to read but isn't essential.
- The chair should ensure that the agenda is followed and that meetings run on time. A good chair makes a huge difference to a meeting. She won't let debates run on and on and will ensure that participants follow the agenda.

- The chair should invite all members to participate in the discussion. The role of the chair is to ensure that no one dominates the meeting and that no one fails to contribute fully.
- All board members should respect the chair's authority.
- Debates should be robust but be conducted in a courteous manner.
- Members' contributions should be relevant and concise, focusing on strategic issues rather than operational matters. You may like the sound of your own voice, but do not drone on and on.
- Members should be happy to accept collective decisions even when they have voted against them. At the end of the meeting, unless you are resigning as a result of the decisions that have been made, you leave the boardroom accepting and acknowledging the collective vote.

BOARD PERFORMANCE HEALTH CHECK

The next improvement process should be a formal annual board health check. Just as a regular personal health check can help prevent potential illness, a board health check can help prevent future problems. Some of the components of good board performance are outlined below and can be used as a quick check that everything is working as it should be.

- Have you got a strategic plan?
- Is your plan well thought-out and actively monitored?
- Are you able to attract new board members as you need them?
- Have you got an appropriate and diverse mix of people, including a variety of skills and ages?
- Have you got a well thought-out and comprehensive board induction programme?
- Have you a clear set of values that all board members can articulate?
- Is your board trained in legal and compliance matters?
- Are board papers available and circulated in a timely manner?
- Do board members contribute to all board matters in an articulate and acceptable manner?

- Are all the vital policies in place for health and safety and risk?

You could use a simple yes/no survey, or use a facilitator and then discuss the answers at an away day. But it is important not to simply pay lip-service to this or it will soon lose its credibility.

For a more in-depth view of board health, especially for a growing or ambitious board, you may like to consider an annual evaluation.

Full board evaluation

The board is responsible for the ongoing monitoring of its own effectiveness. It is hugely valuable to evaluate the board regularly and to manage feedback from all board members and key managers regarding the ongoing effectiveness of the board structure, skills, processes and outputs. There are plenty of evaluation tools you can download from the internet but I am not overly keen on "tick box" evaluations. Generally, if a scoring system is out of five, most scores tend to come out at three or four so don't tell you very much. However, that isn't to say that you shouldn't use them – just use them with care. They are almost always more effective if used in conjunction with board observation by a trained evaluator on board performance.

The benefits

There are undoubtedly a number of benefits to board performance that result from taking part in a performance evaluation process, some of which may include:

- improved leadership
- greater clarity of roles and responsibilities
- improved teamwork
- greater accountability
- better decision-making
- improved communication
- more efficient board operations.

As part of the UK Corporate Governance Code requirements, from 2012 many FTSE 350 companies have had to start preparing for a board evaluation using an external facilitator for the first time.

The problems

Without a third-party facilitator, board evaluations can be very biased. Some board members may use them as an opportunity to criticise their colleagues, while others may wish to do this but do not have the confidence to speak honestly about the situation. It is entirely possible that some board members are simply not aware of certain issues, relating either to themselves or to others. Although it may be possible to hide board flaws from an outside observer, the right person should be able to see beneath the surface.

Unless the board members have all come to the conclusion that this process is necessary and they are totally committed to being open and honest, then the evaluation will not be worthwhile.

MY OWN EXPERIENCE

I was recently speaking at the Association of Women Chartered Secretaries (AWCS) conference and one very experienced evaluator said that one of her chairs had decided to ask the board members only the following two questions for the year's evaluation process and that each member had to answer in between 250 and 500 words.

1. What is the biggest challenge the board is facing this year?
2. What will your biggest contribution to the board's work be this year?

BOARD IMPROVEMENTS

Having the right processes and the right people with the right positive attitude, and supporting them with training or coaching, are all steps in the right direction, but there is nothing that cannot be improved upon. Additional board procedures that should be part of any board's desire to do better are discussed below.

Establishing a board charter

This single document sets out how the board performs its role and is essentially a code of conduct for the board. It can also be part of an induction process for any new board member. The board charter should include the following:

- details of the role of the board in the business
- information on the board members (with mini profiles) and the board composition
- a copy of the reserved powers of the board and any powers reserved to the shareholders
- the board meeting schedule
- a corporate organisation chart
- details of the roles and responsibilities of the board members and officers of the company
- the values and vision and a mission statement
- a code of conduct for directors
- the board dispute process.

In itself, this document is not a remedy for bad behaviour in the boardroom, but provided it is well communicated and kept up to date, it can be invaluable in improving board culture and director communication.

Recognising cultural differences

There are cultural differences in the way people do business around the world, and a well-functioning board of any company with an international profile needs to be sensitive of these. Here are just a few that I have noticed over the years. In all cases they are generalisations, but I have found them to be useful ones.

Power

In some countries, for example Malaysia, you are expected to show proper respect to superiors. In other countries, such as Denmark, differences in organisational rank or social class are regarded as irrelevant.

Certainty versus uncertainty

Germany, for instance, prefers structure and predictability, which results in German directors being more likely to be subject to explicit rules of behaviour and strict laws. On French or Italian boards, a more fluid approach to activity in the boardroom is the norm.

The battle of the sexes

Male-dominated cultures, such as in Japan and China, reflect values such as success, authority, competition and material rewards, which are usually more associated with male roles. In contrast, more feminine cultures, such as in Sweden, focus more on values such as personal relationships, care for others and quality of life.

WHEN THE LUNATICS TAKE OVER THE BOARDROOM

Over the years I have been in some challenging board meetings, even some that have ended in physical fights, and I have certainly witnessed my fair share of screaming and shouting. Sometimes this has been the result of real passion for a particular issue, and sometimes it has been a very personal attack.

The right board mix and balance can definitely help. In my experience, a gender mix creates a more civilised behaviour pattern, as do a great chair and non-executive director.

These are some of the toughest economic times we have had to work in, and as a result the behaviour of many directors has been exaggerated as they try to deal with unforeseen issues. This is a strong argument in favour of regenerating the board mix and encouraging personal development and training.

TRAINING AND QUALIFICATIONS

There are many formal and informal training programmes, but the IoD (www.iod.com) provides director development courses that can lead to a recognised qualification. These are widely recognised as some of the best director training qualifications in the world. They are expensive, but not as expensive as ignorance!

Certificate in Company Direction

According to the IOD:

> "The certificate encompasses the core knowledge and awareness that is necessary to function effectively as a director. As well as covering subjects such as governance, finance, marketing and strategy, the great advantage of studying for this certificate is the added value of mixing with your peers from hugely different businesses and from whom you will certainly learn as much about good board practices as from the formal training and great technical input from the tutors, all of whom are individual specialists."

Diploma in Company Direction and Developing Board Performance

> "Once you have completed the Certificate in Company Direction courses and examination, the Diploma in Company Direction is the next step. This provides an opportunity to put into practice the knowledge gained from the certificate in a realistic and safe environment. It encourages peer group support, challenge and stimulation, mirroring in many ways the operation of a board. During a three-day programme you get the chance to work through a case study and to put into practice your skill sets playing out roles of chair, CEO and FD [finance director]."

Chartered Director

The certificate and diploma programmes culminate in the Chartered Director professional qualification for directors.

> "Chartered directors lead organisations in the private, public or third sectors, at the highest strategic level. If you want to achieve this highly regarded certificate, you will need to demonstrate the expertise and integrity needed to meet the

challenges of business today. If you are looking to enhance your skills and improve your organisation's performance, the Chartered Director is the professional qualification you need."

The IoD is, of course, only one of the many bodies that provide courses in directorship skills, but it is one of only a few that accredit their programmes.

COACHING AND MENTORING

Formal director training might help you to understand the legal implications of your new role and the responsibilities of company boards. But to help you make the behavioural changes, the best solution is to obtain personal support through executive coaching or via the use of an external or internal mentor.

Choosing the right coach or mentor is essential. You need to choose someone you respect, but you must also like them. It is important to meet face to face at least once a month but you also need access to your coach or mentor via the telephone or by email. They need to respect your confidences and require a high level of emotional intelligence. I have always had a coach or mentor of some sort.

MY OWN EXPERIENCE

My coaches and mentors have taught me numerous things, including the painful lesson about not sending an email when in a temper, appearing positive to my team even when I am desperate, and having confidence in my own beliefs and values.

Some arrangements have been more formal than others, but the knowledge that there is someone there who is impartial and who will listen and guide me has been vital to my career.

Some of the areas a coach or mentor may be able to help with include the following.

- What are the challenges of the new role?
- What do your old colleagues expect of you now? This is important if this is an internal promotion to the board.

- How do you handle the change of status and relationships?
- What do your new boardroom colleagues expect of you? And how can you demonstrate your abilities quickly?
- What do customers, suppliers and other stakeholders now expect? Will you be treated differently? Have you got to act differently? Are the expectations higher? If so, how will you meet them?
- How do you handle dual responsibilities as head of department and board member? (This applies to executive directors.)
- What practical steps should you take to improve your awareness, develop new skills, and establish yourself in your new role? Should you have external training? And how will you know if any training is time (and money) well spent?
- Have you got a good work–life balance? If not, how can you deal with this?

Transition coaching or mentoring both before and after your appointment will help you make a successful move into this new role.

MY OWN EXPERIENCE

I have had a number of mentors and their support has helped me through numerous difficult situations, but one moment of support is particularly memorable.

I had a potential staff litigation issue for what was claimed to be constructive dismissal. In my opinion, this was totally without foundation. In these situations emotions can run high and I was ready for a fight. My mentor was calm and controlled and talked me down from my fury. His approach and reality check enabled me to handle what would otherwise have been, without a doubt, a very different outcome. The key was that I could be myself with my mentor and he could tell me what was what in a no-nonsense manner. Because of the huge respect I had for him, it all worked out OK.

Mutual respect, patience, calm and contacts (he put me in touch with a great lawyer) were the keys to this particular door. Thank you, John.

Chapter 5

The first 100 days

"There are people who make things happen, there are people who wait for things to happen and there are people who wonder what happened to them. To be successful you need to be a person who makes things happen."

Jim Lovell, NASA astronaut

Day one has at last arrived and you are filled with hope. Everything seems possible and glowing with potential. Sadly, this feeling can be short-lived. We will cover some of the problems that can arise in Chapter 6, but for now let's look at some ways in which you can make a positive impact in your first few days in the boardroom.

It is important to gain some quick wins and make your mark, whether this is in an executive or a non-executive position. You are often only as good as your last great achievement, and mistakes tend to be remembered longer than achievements.

MY OWN EXPERIENCE

Some of the ways in which I have made an early impact in the boardroom have included renegotiating bank covenants (pre-economic crisis!), opening up my black book of contacts to effect an introduction essential to the businesses, and even something really simple like utilising a proper board agenda (see Chapter 4 and Appendix 3). It doesn't matter what you do, but grab the lowest hanging apple as quickly as possible and then keep on picking them!

So, this chapter will look at how you can ensure that your presence is felt positively from the moment you set foot in reception. We will look at how, by knowing what is expected before you make a move, you are less likely to get it wrong. The chapter will also cover what you must and must not do after the first 100 days to ensure that you keep your position as long as you want, rather than as long as someone else wants!

Some of these activities and suggestions could apply to any senior role, but they are essential for the ambitious director.

DIRECTOR INDUCTION

It has often struck me as rather strange that young graduates joining a business are given a much more structured induction than the new director, particularly considering that it is the director's job to help steer the company to success. This is especially true if the promotion to the board is an internal one. It can seem like one day you are a manager and the next you are a director and expected to direct.

Clearly, this is not ideal for either the company or the new director.

Your chances of success can only be enhanced if the business you are joining does you the courtesy of providing you with a proper induction. If they don't offer one, then it might be a good idea to ask. Although no doubt you will have done your homework before getting to the boardroom, actually being in post probably feels a bit like getting behind the steering wheel of your father's car for the first time after you have passed your driving test. Learning about being a director and being one in practice are very different.

While much can be gleaned from various websites, nothing beats face-to-face meetings with the rest of the board, as well as meeting external critical stakeholders including funders, relevant regulators, lawyers, accountants and key shareholders. Of course, this all depends on the size of the company and board you are joining.

A "buddying" system with another board member can be extremely valuable, and, of course, go and talk to staff at all levels.

The new director checklist in Appendix 6 shows you some of the things you may like to consider for a thorough induction. It isn't an exhaustive list, but it will give you an idea of who does what, where and when, and what not to do.

HOW TO MAKE A GOOD EARLY IMPRESSION

Once in post, every personal encounter counts in the early days, so make an impact as quickly as possible.

Here are a few points to consider.

Have a chameleon-like personality
The ability to adapt to your board is vital. That is not to say that you shouldn't be yourself – you absolutely should! – but, as any neuro-linguistic programming practitioner will tell you, understanding how your peer group works and "mirroring" them when needed will undoubtedly help speed up your integration into the "club".

Don't be a Dementor
For those who haven't read the Harry Potter stories, Dementors suck away the positivity and happiness in those they touch. We have all met negative people who will always find fault in even the most positive of situations. If you have spent any time at all working with such types, you will know how draining the whole situation becomes and it is very likely you will start to avoid them.

I am not suggesting that an unreasonable amount of bonhomie is always appropriate, but I do know that having a positive mindset will make you and those around you more inclined to succeed.

Make an impact in meetings
Having the right ideas is not enough. You need to present them well and follow them up.

Speak clearly and have well thought-out arguments. Be prepared to listen to other views and don't be defensive. Speak with authority and conviction and be prepared to defend you position, but never to the point of obstinacy.

You need to show those who sit around the board table with you that you are pleased to be there and have much to offer. At the same time, you need to read the situation and personalities so that you can adapt your approach.

Don't be afraid to voice your convictions and be prepared to provide evidence if needed.

You might make a mistake – anyone can – but if you do, own up quickly and learn from it. *Never* blame someone else.

Understand the job role

What does the board want from you and when, and how can you be sure that you are meeting those expectations? If you are in any doubt, ask for clarification and for feedback. Ask what the key issues are and what the board is doing about them, and then consider how you can support or add to this process. Stand up, stand out and make things happen – you cannot afford to watch from the sidelines. Know that you are a director.

Get to know the team

The team isn't just the other board members; it includes the people who execute the board's decisions and the support staff. I have found that I often get to know more about the business I am working in from further down the management line than I do from my peers.

There are no stupid questions, so don't be afraid to ask. You will be much more effective if you accumulate knowledge about the business quickly. Some information will be volunteered but a lot of information won't be, so tune into the business chatter (but steer clear of the gossip).

Understand the market in which you operate

There has never been as much global economic change as there is now. The world is smaller than ever before and technologically is advancing at an alarming rate. You cannot overlook new markets, especially in the BRIC countries (Brazil, Russia, India and China), whatever field you operate in. Your customers will be more demanding than ever and you need to be proactive about keeping ahead of what they might want.

Be careful about doing the unexpected

When a new director arrives in any company, sometimes the staff are looking for signs of reassurance to lessen their uncertainty, so don't try to change too much in your first week.

Be positive

It is easy to be critical of whoever was in the role before you. After all, they are an easy target. But be wary about doing this. It gives the impression that you are the type of person who passes the buck, blames others and is insincere. So, make positive comments while acknowledging possible shortcomings in the past.

Listen, listen and listen some more

If you are new to any senior post, there will be all sorts of people coming to you with issues and concerns and looking for you to wave a magic wand. My advice is that you shouldn't make any changes too quickly – it takes time to see the full picture and you need to hear a variety of views.

Seek out the positives and watch for the negatives

Listen to and build on what is going right. You may be at the sharp end of complaints but the staff should also want to share the positives. If they don't, go and look for them. Seek out good performance wherever it is and however small it may be. Show your appreciation – it will be welcomed as long as it is sincere.

Find out what people want

A great thing to ask your team (if you are an executive director) is what one thing they would like to change about the place where they work. Often it is the very small things that can make a substantial difference: a water fountain in the corridor, a better blend of coffee, or perhaps a degree of flexible working.

Of course, you won't be able to do everything they want, and perhaps you won't be able to do anything at all. However, whatever you can or can't do, take the time to explain to your team what you are doing.

Have fun, be kind, stay positive and work hard

These are my personal and work values and have helped me through challenging times. They are not always easy to adhere to – particularly staying positive – but I do my best.

What I have learned is that a negative attitude at the top pretty soon escalates downwards, which is hugely damaging on morale and business output. If I feel I cannot sustain a positive attitude, I leave the building, go for a walk, listen to some music and reflect on some positives. Some time out always helps. As a director you set the tone for the business, so make sure the tone is a good one.

Don't think you know everything

If, for example, you were just promoted to production director from production manager, you may feel you know everything about production. Even if that is true (and it almost certainly isn't), you won't know everything about the most important part of your new job, which is helping improve the whole business. Listen to the people around you. Ask for their input when appropriate. Keep an open mind.

Don't turn into a megalomaniac

Everyone in the company will know who the new director is, so you don't have to make a big show about being "the boss". You do, however, have to demonstrate that, as the boss, you are making a positive difference.

Don't be afraid to do things

Maybe you didn't ask for the promotion. Maybe you are not sure you can do the job. Don't let that keep you from doing it to the very best of your abilities. Doing nothing is never the answer. If you feel you need training, ask for it, even if it means you have to contribute time and even money.

MY OWN EXPERIENCE

It was my first major negotiation meeting in my role as finance director. On the other side of the table sat a highly experienced team of merger and acquisitions people, some of whom were at least twice my age at the time, and all male (naturally). Was I scared? Of course I was, but actually in hindsight my age, my gender and my naivety worked in my favour. They underestimated me and were condescending, whereas I – because of my fear and possibly also my paranoia – had researched them all thoroughly, including their weak spots. I had developed, in the words of *Blackadder*'s Baldrick, a "cunning plan", which they didn't see coming at all!

Take responsibility

You are now where the buck stops, so even if it isn't your fault or even in your area of expertise, you must help resolve problems that the company is facing. You won't necessarily have to solve the issues on your own, but you certainly will have to do so with your fellow directors. The board is the last bastion of blame and resolution; you are part of that team and must step up to the mark.

Don't forget that by law you must always act in the best interests of the company, and you also have to behave with honesty. Decisiveness is now vital, so don't dither unnecessarily. Sometimes you have to make a decision even if ultimately it isn't a great one.

CHECKLIST FOR THE FIRST 100 DAYS

As a member of the board of directors, don't forget that you are responsible for governing the business, so you need to ensure that it can carry out its mission and that it does so legally, ethically and effectively. Ultimately, the board is accountable to all the business's stakeholders.

As a member of the board, you must know good governance practices so that the board can fulfil its primary mission while remaining transparent, accountable and legitimate.

Get to grips with the business strategy and business plan

You need to be able to recite the values of the business with conviction and have a clear understanding of its strategic goals.

Check the funding and human resources

Look at funding agreements and make yourself entirely familiar and comfortable with the covenants. Check that the staff engagement is the best it can be. If you feel there are gaps, ask for clarification of the actions to be taken.

Read and understand the management and financial accounts

You need to review the last three years' financial accounts and the up-to-date accounts against budgets and forecasts. You should look at trends and key performance indicators and always question inconsistencies. All board members are responsible for the board's decisions and actions, whether or not they attend every meeting, and financial illiteracy is no excuse. If your understanding of financial matters is poor, get some training now.

Check critical policies

Read, review and ask for clarification of the key business policies. These include but are not limited to:

- health and safety
- risk
- compliance (e.g. with Financial Services Authority rules)
- equal opportunities
- customer care
- bribery and corruption
- auditing and accounting
- supplier engagement
- employment policies such as on disciplinary procedures and dispute management
- supplier contracts.

Get out and about

You need to meet your stakeholders; these include customers, suppliers, staff and funders.

Depending on your area of business, you may also want to get better acquainted with the local community, which may be a source of support if treated with respect. The local area may also provide your next tranche of employees, or even your customer base, so don't ignore it.

Act ethically and honestly

Although business ethics can vary from one company to another, honesty is a clearly understood value.

All board members are responsible for the behaviour of their colleagues. If you feel at any point that matters are being dealt with in a way that is less than 100% honest, then you should make this known to the rest of the board. If the issue is particularly serious, you should contact the police. There are protective legal instruments for what is known as whistleblowing. I would hope that this is not a situation you encounter, but your responsibility in such matters is unequivocally to deal with them effectively and immediately.

There are three fundamental principles of good corporate governance:

- accountability, i.e. you will be accountable for your actions
- transparency, i.e. you will be seen to be doing the right thing at the right time
- probity, i.e. you will act honestly and fairly.

Make sure your behaviour as a director adheres to these principles.

Hold regular meetings

If your board meetings are held only quarterly, it could be some time before there is a formal board meeting. If this is the case, it may be worth having an earlier informal meeting of the directors for a general update. In the meantime, get hold of the last six months' board meeting minutes, read and absorb them.

Communicate

The relationship between the board and the executive team can be a difficult one if not managed correctly. Nearly always, problems arise through poor communication on both sides and the difficulty some boards have with not being able to avoid interfering in operational activities.

Here are a couple of tips for building a good relationship between your board and the management team. Introduce them as soon as you are able to.

- Have clear roles and responsibilities mapped out and communicated at all levels. This is best done in writing and, importantly, it must be kept up to date, as roles and responsibilities will evolve.
- Keep away from the operational activities of the management team. Your job is to delegate and support, not to run the department or project. Having said that, it is also important to know when help is required, whether asked for or not, so directors need to learn quickly what questions they should ask.

Remember your legal duties

It has been said that you can't please all of the people all of the time, but what you can do is ensure that you maintain your legal duty to *"promote the success of the business for the benefit of the stakeholders"*. That may well require you to take tough decisions, from losing staff to changing to an international, rather than a local, supplier, but if you keep the legal principles in mind, you are at the very least doing the best you can and acting with care and skill, which is also a legal requirement.

MY OWN EXPERIENCE

Bravely, when I joined a board many years ago I tried the following initiative.

I asked everyone in the company to write on a colour chart. On the red card they wrote down all the things they thought the company should stop doing, on the amber card the things it should start doing, and on the green card all the things it should do more of. I got some interesting comments! But what it gave me was a clear idea from the inside of what the employees thought was required – and it helped me create a great business plan quickly.

Chapter 6

Office and boardroom politics

"Arguing with a fool proves there are two."
Doris M. Smith

This chapter will look at the demons and assassins that you will find in many boardrooms. It will seek to equip you with the tools to keep these destructive forces at bay.

Having fought so hard to get a board position, few would want to give up easily. However, sometimes, as they say, "if you can't change the people, you need to change the people". By that, I mean that usually it is appropriate to work with people to try to improve or change their behaviour, but sometimes this just isn't possible. If this really does prove to be the case, then perhaps the board needs new people.

There is a certain British mentality that it is almost a sin to be successful. Unlike the American dream of owning your own home and being independently wealthy, we Brits have been brought up to be more reserved about our achievements. In fact, many very successful people suffer from "impostor syndrome", that overwhelming feeling of doubt when a little voice in your head shouts: "I am a fraud ... I am about to be caught out ... I really shouldn't be here." Sadly, because many "impostors" have unsustainably high standards, they often set themselves up to fail. And if on top of this there is someone waiting in the wings with a dagger or two, you can see how life for the aspirational director can get a bit hairy at times, to say the least!

You are a lucky woman or man if you love everyone you work with and agree with their every word, every day of your career. At some point or other you will almost certainly meet someone you don't get on with and often, for no apparent reason, you simply find yourself under attack.

Assuming that such attacks are not justified (and, frankly, in my opinion an attack is rarely justified), it is very important for both your career and your personal health that you deal with matters in the correct way. The trouble is that you cannot judge what a company, or indeed a board, is really like until you actually have your feet firmly under the desk. If you are not going to roll over, or walk away as soon as things get difficult, you will need some survival tips.

BOARDROOM SURVIVAL TIPS

Tip 1

There is not a single company I have worked in where there hasn't been a clique of some sort. My experience is that you are either inside or outside this group. The situation has often reminded me of my school days, when you were either one of the popular people or one of the less than popular ones. I was never one of the popular ones, and at the time this upset me; I felt genuinely excluded. Now I can normally rise above it. I am not saying that this is easy, particularly if you feel excluded from a peer group, but it is an important skill to develop. Men are generally much better at this than women, who tend to be more inclined to take a personal comment to heart. In my experience, more often than not the man doesn't even hear it!

Tip 2

It is important for a director to be friendly but not *friends* with the people who work for her. This is an important distinction. It isn't always easy, particularly if this is an internal promotion, but I know from very bitter experience that if you have crossed this line and you later need to discipline the "friend", or worse remove them from their post, it is an unenviable task for all but the most ruthless of directors.

Tip 3

Don't listen to the devils and demons in the business. There are some people for whom doom and gloom is a way of life. Don't get sucked into this, as you will find yourself on a downward spiral. Never mind half full or half empty, I have always been a "glass overflowing" sort of person, but constant, relentless negative behaviour can bring anyone down, however optimistic they usually are.

Tip 4

Keep an eye on your work–life balance. This is a tip I wish I was better at following myself. Every evening, as I drag myself out of the office once again at 7pm, I remind myself of the old saying that no one ever wishes on their deathbed that they had spent more time in the office. Now, as I've entered my fifth decade, I can only reflect on the things I haven't done because I gave too much time to work.

Tip 5

If you do find yourself working long hours, and sometimes it is unavoidable, be sure you at least set aside some "me time". For me this would be a trip to the shops or the beauticians, or even to the gym. Whatever it is for you, schedule some time for it, and stick to it just as you would if it were an important meeting. This will help you avoid turning into one of those unpleasant, destructive forces you are seeking to avoid.

Tip 6

Bullying, unfortunately, can occur in the boardroom just as it can in any workplace. Sometimes it is because of jealousy, sometimes a malicious personality – whatever the excuse, it is never justified and you must be adept at rising above it.

If the bully's nastiness is directed at you, and you can't think of a witty retort, smile sweetly and thank them for being so honest. There is often no better way to disarm an enemy than by countering their hostility with friendliness. It has worked for me countless times in such situations. As Oscar Wilde said: *"Always forgive your enemies, nothing annoys them so much."*

Don't be tempted to curry the bully's favour to get an easy life. You will lose the respect and support of the rest of your board. Remember: wolves hunt in packs, and you wouldn't want to give the bully extra strength.

MY OWN EXPERIENCE

Wherever possible, my rule is to smile and laugh things off. It's disarming (so I have been told) and effective when used properly. But it doesn't always work. Hard as I try not to rise to anyone's bait, I don't always succeed – and I always regret it when I don't. In those cases, a short trip to the loo, a few stamps of the feet and a silent scream are very therapeutic. And if that doesn't work, there's always the voodoo doll I keep at home . . .

IS IT ME?

As much as I would like to pretend it never happens, sadly some of us (and I include myself) sometimes just take an instant dislike to another person, more often than not for no reason.

This doesn't happen too often and when it does I am quite conscious of it. I may have smiled at the person in question and they haven't responded in the same way, or it could have been an off-the-cuff remark they made. The trouble is that once this has happened, I find it difficult to address them. No matter what they do, I can't shake off the dislike.

This is, of course, very self-destructive. Worse still, I have been known to brood over the matter, sometimes for days. This is made even more difficult when someone else tells me how charming, able and intelligent my dislikeable colleague is.

Because this is generally a pointless exercise, I am learning to put these sorts of feelings behind me. If it turns out that my intuition was in fact correct, as it occasionally is, then I have found that patience is a wonderful thing – more often than not, that person has been found wanting by someone else and has disappeared from my radar.

Prevention is preferable to cure, so although it is always sensible to adopt a positive stance when joining a board, you should always be prepared for possible conflicts. That isn't to say that you should begin by distrusting your fellow board members – far from it – but you should approach a new board with a healthy degree of caution.

BE POSITIVE AND DON'T WORRY

Avoid the doom merchants

As I have mentioned before, one of my values is the ability to stay positive. I'm a bit like Pollyanna in the children's book – I'm a naturally optimistic person. However, I am aware that when I work with or for people who have a less positive attitude than my own, it can be easy to slip into a more negative state of mind.

It takes a strong mindset to constantly push back against negativity, but push back you must. As a director, you should not be a merchant of doom and treat every problem as a major setback; rather, you need to see them as opportunities to make a particular situation better. We all know that dealing with a customer complaint in the right way can turn a disastrous situation into a very positive piece of PR. I have seen it done on several occasions, for example when I have had to return a product to a shop or have had a poor meal in a restaurant.

Don't hide from the problems

Although you should have a positive mindset, that doesn't mean you should ignore critical issues. As tempting as it may be to hope that things will go away or that someone else will sort them out, as a director you should now be fully aware that any ramifications of not dealing with a problem will be the responsibility of you and your fellow board members.

Almost without exception, every day will bring you a new set of problems, whether they relate to a customer, staff or supplier issue. Years ago I would park these difficulties and deal with the more pleasant aspects of my role first, but age and experience have taught me that it is far better to tackle the more challenging issues first. Not only will you be at your freshest, but once you have dealt with those challenges, other issues can be tackled correctly and swiftly. I find that the sense of satisfaction I get from dealing with the most difficult problem first allows me to tackle the next issue with renewed vigour.

One tip is to keep a running list of tasks that need addressing, update it daily, delegate the easy things and tackle the big issues first. You will find you get a lot of satisfaction just from crossing items off the list. Don't forget that a great director knows how to prioritise and how to delegate but must never abdicate responsibility.

Don't worry about things that can't be fixed

Some issues you encounter cannot be fixed, or at least not immediately. Worrying about them will not make the situation better, nor will it make the problems go away. I have had countless sleepless nights brooding over matters that were beyond my control; all the worry achieved was a negative impact on both my health and my ability to deal with the matters I *could* control.

If you are a control freak – and many successful people are – you might find it useful to write these worries down in the back of a small book with a date against them. I carry a book like this with me at all times, and it helps me to look back at it, sometimes months later, when the issues are usually no longer relevant. I tend to find that either the problem has been resolved by circumstances or something more positive has superseded it.

It doesn't matter what your coping mechanism is, but you will need one. Whatever it is you are worrying about will have little or no relevance in 100 years' time. So concentrate on fixing the things you can deal with and leave those you can't to fate.

DON'T ALLOW YOURSELF TO BE ATTACKED

This can happen — you may not see it coming, but suddenly you are under attack. The attack can come from a colleague, a customer, a supplier, or indeed any internal or external force.

It is rarely justified to attack another person verbally in private — and never, ever in public. Some people in high positions are simply bullies, some have allowed the power to go to their heads, and some are simply bad-tempered. If you find yourself on the end of a wholly unjustified public or private attack (as I have on occasion), then your natural reaction will be one of either flight or fight. In my case, rightly or wrongly, it is usually the latter. Attack me and I become defensive and fight my corner, but this is hard work and emotionally draining so I have developed some coping techniques.

It is very disarming indeed to say nothing at all to your attackers. Let them talk until they have nothing more to say. It is also very effective to stay calm. Nothing annoys a bully more than a lack of response. At the end of a rant, I might say, "So is that it?" Very often, of course, this starts them off again and once again the key is to stay quiet and calm until they have finished. I have often found that this method of dealing with an attack lets the person talk themselves out, and often they start to say things like, "Well, I guess it wasn't all your fault."

There are, of course, occasions when there may be some substance to the content of the attack. Maybe you have made a serious mistake. The fact remains that a seething rant is not the way to handle these matters. If the issue is genuine, I would still suggest that it is best handled by being passive during the attack. Then, when the individual has calmed down, use a measured tone to repeat back to them what you have understood to be the issue. Once you have both agreed this — and it is important that there is absolute clarity about the issue in question — then discuss how you will tackle the problem.

The key to dealing with these attacks is to stay very calm, in both your body language and your tone of voice.

MY OWN EXPERIENCE

I was recently "attacked" in a negotiation meeting. I was ready to flare into counteroffensive mode but I dug my rather long nails into my hands to physically prevent this. The provoker in question had "waggled his horns" at me from the first moment we met, announcing himself as senior partner and asking in a condescending manner if I worked alone, suggesting I was a one-man band and his operation far superior to mine, and that I might be out of my depth playing with the "big boys".

Smiling broadly, as I have mentioned, is very effective. I could see immediately that he was disarmed and I did nothing to dispel his incorrect belief.

Being from Yorkshire and being blonde means that I am often underestimated – to some people it does perhaps suggest a lack of intelligence. I have always seen this as a massive advantage, as my opponents often don't see me coming. In this particular case it worked exactly in my favour and I secured a much better deal than I was expecting. I kept calm in the meeting and I know that helped. Yes, I might have gone into the ladies' room and done a little foot stamping, but my antagonist was never to know that.

The secret assassins

Not everyone who comes to attack you is wearing a black leather jacket and carrying a violin case. They often come disguised as friends and even family. This section of the book is not meant to suggest that you should trust no one, but rather that in business you should adopt a certain amount of caution before you let your guard down completely. Here are a few characters you might meet in and outside the boardroom.

The sarcastic one

I detest sarcastic people; sarcasm is the lowest form of wit. I find that these people can often dish it out but can rarely take it if such comments are directed at them.

The shark

Waiting in the wings for you to make a mistake, however minor, this person plants carefully thought-out seeds of doubt in your mind about your ability.

The "frenemy"

This is a person who seems to be on your side. She has backed you on a project, either outside or in the boardroom, but she has a hidden agenda and is waiting for the right moment to publicly undermine you.

The ambitious one

She wants the top job, maybe even your job, and nothing is going to stop her. She will use whatever means she has at her disposal to undermine and outsmart you. She takes no prisoners and makes her goals very clear, but she is the easiest of these characters to deal with because she doesn't hide her intentions.

MY OWN EXPERIENCE

Over the years I have encountered my fair share of difficult people. Before I grew a thicker skin and a few grey hairs, I found this all very upsetting. Now I take it as an unfortunate but inevitable part of business. I have developed a very effective antenna and take a while to trust people. I know some of you reading this will say "how sad", but trust, I find, is more sustainable if it is hard-won.

TIPS FOR DEALING WITH DIFFICULT PEOPLE

It is all very well to be able to identify these people who will sabotage your confidence, but it is also important to know how to deal with them.

Stay calm

I have already said how important it is to appear calm. You may well be seething inside but you must not show it. Losing your temper with the other person is rarely the best way to get her to collaborate with you. Unless you know that anger will trigger the person into action and you are consciously using it as a strategy, it is better to assume a calm persona. I call it killing with kindness.

Be empathetic and listen

Approach any discussion in an informed and temperate way and listen to what the other person is saying. Often when we have got close to a resolution, I have realised, as has the other party, that we probably would have resolved the problem more quickly and smoothly if we had adopted the correct approach from the start.

Share your concerns

Worrying about the particular person won't make them go away. It can help to talk, but be careful how you go about this and who you talk to. The last thing you want is to appear to be a gossip. I have mentioned previously the value of an external mentor or coach, and if you are fortunate enough to have one they may be the best person to confide in. If the situation is increasingly difficult and nothing is working, you may well have to escalate the matter to HR, or, if there is no suitable HR person, to the MD or chair.

Tell your side of the story

One thing that has worked for me is letting the person know the reasons for my position. Sometimes they are being resistant because they think that *you* are being difficult with them. Explaining the reasons behind your actions and the full background of what is happening will enable them to empathise with your situation. This helps them to get on board much more easily.

Talk to them

Dealing with a delicate situation by email or text is wholly inappropriate and, frankly, cowardly. The tone is rarely interpreted correctly and there is no opportunity to build rapport.

It is also much more effective to deal with such situations on neutral territory. Get out of the office and go somewhere quiet where you can both talk without fear of interruption.

Be courteous

Of course, this should be a given, but tempers fray and we can all lash out. The problem is that it is difficult to retract what has been said, and we have a tendency to hear only the bad things. As the golden rule says: *"Do unto others as you would have them do unto you."*

Agree a time frame for resolution

Not all problems can be resolved immediately, and sometimes the sensible option is to let things cool off a little and return to them later. But if you do this, set a timescale for returning to the issue, and make sure this timescale is agreed upon and adhered to.

Move on

Sometimes, but hopefully not too often, there are issues and situations than cannot be resolved to the satisfaction of both parties. Provided you are comfortable that you have tried everything possible, there comes a point when there is little option but to move on and to put the issue behind you. This is easier said than done, but if there is truly nothing else to be done, it is sometimes the only option.

In this situation, probably the best thing you can do is try to identify what caused the issue in the first place and see if you can put measures in place to ensure that it does not happen again.

MY OWN EXPERIENCE

I have had to escalate issues to a higher authority on several times in previous jobs. Here is one example.

I was sitting on one particular board as financial director and I had grave concerns about the sales director's pricing strategy. Having tried and failed to resolve the issue with the person in question, I reluctantly had a discreet word with the CEO, bringing what I believed was valid data to support my case. This wasn't pleasant for any of us, but I would like to think I was trying to do the best for the company – although the sales director may not have seen it that way!

HANDLING DIFFICULT CONVERSATIONS

When things come to a head, often the only way of moving matters forward is to have a face-to-face conversation with the individual concerned about their performance and behaviour. These things are never pleasant, but often the anticipation is worse than the reality. In fact, these conversations have the potential to be constructive if handled properly.

So here are my tips.

Don't speak to people in the corridor

Think about the location and the time before sitting down to discuss something difficult. It is best to avoid 5pm on a Friday or 9am on a Monday. Nor will such a conversation ever be effective if either party has limited time. Location also matters – somewhere quiet, private and off-site is usually best.

MY OWN EXPERIENCE

Finding the perfect time usually depends on the case in question, but as a general rule *wait* – ask in advance for a meeting and don't just jump straight into a conversation. Evenings work best for me but I avoid Fridays. I always base my judgement on the individual concerned. I have found that if you can create the right circumstances for the conversation you improve the chances of a good reaction.

Start with a positive comment

"I want us to be able to resolve this together." "We will find a way to sort this out." Repeat these phrases throughout the conversation and celebrate every step towards agreement. Keep summarising, partly so that the other party can see that progress is being made, but also to make sure that they understand what has been agreed. Keep your tone of voice calm and at a moderate volume. Smile!

Don't dismiss the other person's point of view

Just because their view isn't the same as yours doesn't necessarily mean it is incorrect. It certainly won't feel incorrect to them. Use phrases such as "I hear what you are saying", "I understand how you feel about this". This way the other person will not feel threatened and is more likely to be open. Make sure that these phrases don't sound like hollow platitudes and *do not* follow such statements with the word "but".

Stick to the facts

Personal remarks are never positive, nor are emotional outbursts. Similarly, caustic remarks and sarcastic comments only fuel the fury. Don't get angry and make sure you don't cry. If you feel that things are getting out of hand, ask for a break to compose yourself. It is very important not to overreact, or to speak before you have thought through the implications of a misplaced word. Celebrate every small positive movement; use phrases such as "I am so pleased we have agreed on this point".

Create the right atmosphere

Launching straight into the issue won't be effective. Use simple, courteous comments such as "Thank you for taking time out of your schedule. I know we are all very busy." Small talk may seem trite if the issue is very serious, but it does help put people at ease.

Use your eyes and your ears

Watching how people react physically to a comment can be very telling. You do not have to be an expert in body language to realise that if someone sits with their arms crossed they are being defensive, and if they turn away from you in a conversation they are probably not as engaged as they could be. If you are attuned to this then you need to deal with it. Use phrases such as "Are you OK with this?", "Do you have another suggestion?" or "I can see this isn't what you would wish for, so what else could we do?"

Focus on future goals

Agree on the end goal at the start of the meeting. You may not get there, of course, but by agreeing exactly what it is that both of you are trying to resolve, both parties can work towards a mutually desired objective. Keep coming back to this objective and reaffirming it throughout the meeting.

Don't stop listening

Show that you are listening to the other person by repeating back to them your understanding of what they have said. Use phrases such as "So as I understand it your point is ..." or "For clarity can I just confirm that my understanding of your issue is ..." Don't be insincere. Smile appropriately when engaging in the conversation and use plenty of eye contact.

Conclude with a summary of the meeting

It is essential that both parties leave the room with a clear understanding of what has been agreed. Ideally, any verbal agreement should always be put in writing. The written summary should be circulated as soon as possible after the meeting and provided to everyone concerned to confirm their mutual understanding.

On occasion I have seen this used as a way of putting in writing what one party wanted rather than what was actually agreed. Don't be tempted to do this. If you have worked hard to achieve progress, this sort of devious behaviour will set you back further than where you were at the start of the process.

DISCRIMINATION AND HOW TO DEAL WITH IT

MY OWN EXPERIENCE

In 25 years in the boardroom, I have only rarely faced overt discrimination. In one of my early roles in a Yorkshire textile mill, whose name is long forgotten to all but those who worked there, the MD took me to one side on the first day in my post as finance director (the only woman on the board) and said he thought the other directors (all male, pale and grey) would be uncomfortable if I joined them for lunch.

For the whole of the six months I was in post (which was as long as I could take it, as this was the start of a long litany of subtle discrimination and bullying), I never once ate lunch in the office. I would leave the premises to have lunch, even once sitting in the ladies' loo, as I appeared to be unwelcome in the canteen and definitely not wanted at the directors' table.

The days of such overt sexism are long gone for most companies, I'm pleased to say, but discrimination comes in many guises. With age and the growth of a much thicker skin, I'd be able to laugh off such behaviour, but this has only come with time.

You may say, why should you suffer? After all, discrimination is against the law. My advice would be to choose your battles carefully in order to win the war.

The final hurdle to your dream position is sometimes not anything you have or haven't done, but the colour of your skin, your gender or your weight. Stereotyping still exists, even though overt discrimination on such grounds as age, race, sex or sexuality is outlawed and can be challenged in law.

If you recognise or suspect that you have a tendency towards this type of behaviour yourself, you need to take positive action to stop yourself. Not least because there is a presumption of guilt in discrimination cases. If you end up in court, the burden is on you to prove that you haven't been discriminating.

If you are the victim, your right to protection from discrimination applies even if you have not been employed as yet by the perpetrator. Discrimination has no limit on claims and can include claims for hurt feelings.

Discrimination in the workplace

Legislation exists to prevent discrimination on the following grounds:

- age
- colour
- disability
- ethnic background
- gender
- gender reassignment
- marriage or civil partnership
- nationality
- pregnancy and maternity leave
- race
- religion or belief
- sexual orientation.

But what does this mean in practice?

Direct discrimination

This is when an employer treats one employee less favourably than another on one or more of the grounds mentioned above. In general, this is always illegal, but there are limited, rare circumstances in which an employer might be able to make a case for a genuine occupational requirement, for example that a blind person cannot be a chauffeur.

Indirect discrimination

This is when a working condition or a business rule disadvantages one group of people more than another. For example, an obligation for all employees to go to business social functions might discriminate against those whose religious beliefs forbade this. If an employee's chances of promotion were affected by this, it would be indirect discrimination.

Harassment

At work, or even in a work-related setting such as an office party, any comment that the injured party feels is offensive could be classed as harassment. What is important here is whether the individual concerned thinks that they have been harassed; what may seem like office banter to you may not be regarded as such by the claimant.

How to overcome discrimination and bullying at work

There are many factors that affect career advancement. Here are a few things to consider as you navigate your way to the top.

- Don't assume that the reason why you're not getting ahead is because of your race, sex, age, or any other characteristic. Make sure that your personal goals are aligned with current organisational priorities. Be absolutely sure that you have been unfairly discriminated against before you take action.
- If you feel that you are being bullied or discriminated against at work, keep a log of everything, however small the issue. Often it isn't individual incidents, which can be very minor and petty in themselves, that constitute discrimination, but the sheer volume of such incidents over time.
- If you have anything in writing that could potentially be evidence of discrimination or classed as harassment, then keep copies of it. Years ago, after I had been mugged on holiday and my BlackBerry was stolen and I had to buy another, the memo from my then MD about the incident was all about how he hoped I would reimburse the company once the insurance paid out. In the end I put the matter behind me and moved on, but had I wanted to lodge a claim for unfair treatment that memo would have been useful.

MOVING ON OR MOVING OUT

There comes a point in all our careers, even if you are at the top of the ladder, when you have to make a decision: move on or move out.

MY OWN EXPERIENCE

There have been two occasions when, within a very short time, I have realised that I have made a bad move. On both occasions it was a cultural clash. Moving on was very difficult as rapid mobility from post to post, especially 15 years ago, was not a positive career move. However, in retrospect, I should have moved much more quickly on both occasions.

When to fight and when to surrender

Sometimes we just need to surrender and let events run their course. So how do we choose when to fight and when to surrender? However bad things are, you may have no choice but to stay in post, albeit for a short time while you make other plans. Some things are easier to do than others, but here are a few ideas to help you ride out the storm.

Keep telling yourself you can rise above it

Some people find this easier than others. When undesirable things of this nature have happened to me, I tell myself that the other person is small-minded and needs to get a life, but I can't deny that it does hurt personally.

Stay positive

Take an audit of your life – and have the positive mindset of a Pollyanna. Think about what you have and what others don't have. You are fortunate indeed!

Network like crazy

Networking is a chore for most people – I can drink only so much warm Chablis, then I am ready to leave – but it is an essential part of business life, so always make use of any networking events to which you are invited.

Always have plan B

I don't have a trust fund and not much of a nest egg, but I do have another plan in mind if things don't go according to plan A.

Time to move on

If you notice any of the following key signs, it is probably time to move on.

You are bored
Each day seems to drag on, the work is no longer a challenge, and you can see nothing ahead that is likely to improve.

There is nowhere else to go to
If you remain ambitious and are at the top of the particular company tree and yet you still don't feel fulfilled, it is perhaps the right time to look outside the business for other opportunities. This is never easy if you have been in post or at the same company for some time, but if your ambitions cannot be satisfied within the business, it is time to look elsewhere.

Your stress levels are unacceptable
Being a director comes with a certain amount of stress. Of course, some people are better at handling huge amounts of stress than others, but everyone has only so much capacity. There comes a point when it isn't worth your health, let alone the company's performance, to exceed those stress levels for any length of time.

You are being kept in the dark
Perhaps you are being excluded on purpose. Perhaps you are being sidelined. If you are being kept in the dark deliberately, you need to find out why. If the problem is insurmountable and your exclusion is just a ruse to move you out, you can deal with it in two ways.

- Fight your corner, and seek legal advice if necessary.
- Move out of the company and on to a better one.

Every day is a struggle
If you dread every day in the office or workplace, something is terribly wrong. We all have bad days, but if every day is a bad one you mustn't put up with the situation indefinitely.

You don't feel comfortable in your role
Perhaps the role is not what you expected, or perhaps in your heart of hearts you know you are not up to it, but if you sense that things are not working out then you mustn't stay and fester. Move on quickly as staying will only dent your confidence further.

Before you take any decision

Whatever your age or situation, you need to take a long hard look at your current role and ask yourself the following questions.

Am I really doing the job I want to do?

I have had the odd career crisis. When I was 40 I took six months out of my business and trained to be an aromatherapist! It wasn't for me, but I needed to see what life looked like on the other side of the fence.

I was fortunate in that I had my own business and could afford to try something else. If you are not so lucky, try volunteering – it could open your eyes to different opportunities.

Is there sufficient challenge?

Life can be very dull if you are dealing with the same issues every day. If that is the case, then do something about it. I get bored very easily; I need constant challenges and like nothing better than a problem. In fact, my staff say that I look for them. That is why I have started three new businesses in the last two years.

Could I do better somewhere else?

Well, I guess you will never know until you try, but leaving a comfortable position takes guts and a determination to succeed. Years ago it was acceptable, and indeed preferable, to stay with one company for your whole life. Things have changed now and a more fluid CV is actually desirable.

FOREWARNED IS FOREARMED

So, to sum up, an excuse to do nothing is not an excuse. Choose your battles. *"You got to know when to hold 'em, know when to fold 'em, know when to walk away, know when to run,"* as Kenny Rogers sang in "The Gambler".

Finally: never send emails in anger – they cannot be retracted. Never lose your cool. Control is the winning ingredient.

Chapter 7

Board improvements and barriers to change

"I have always respected those who try to change the
world for the better rather than just complain about it."
Michael Bloomberg

As we approach the end of this book, it is appropriate to consider, in a
broader sense, what needs to be done nationally and internationally to
improve corporate governance for everyone, for their businesses, and
especially for women all over the world.

This chapter will explore the changes that are being seen and those that
we still need to explore. It will examine what is practical and realistic
and what still remains a pipe dream. Its aim is to leave you with the key
question: *How can I be part of the important changes?*

MY OWN EXPERIENCE

I can honestly say I have never ever wanted to be male (not that I am
sexist or believe that one sex is particularly better than the other).
Indeed, I have found it an advantage to be female. Being called Jo, there
have been numerous times when clients and new colleagues have
expected a man in negotiations.

That does not mean that everyone feels the same as me. Many women and minority groups do feel threatened and believe that others can take a prejudiced position against them. As confidently as I may present myself, it is my mission to help those who are not so self-sufficient.

As Madeleine Albright was widely reported as saying: *"There is a special place in hell for women who don't help other women."*

THE FEMALE PERSPECTIVE

"They want the superstar women but are
very happy to have beta men."
Lady de Rothschild

The boardrooms of the world have been evolving, particularly over the last 10 years, but it is a slow process. My mother, who was a successful businesswoman well ahead of her time, told me that change would come in my lifetime. I used to believe her – now I'm not so sure.

Some countries seem to be getting a more balanced perspective sooner than others. Sadly, Britain is not among the front runners.

European Commissioner Viviane Reding proudly announced on 14 November 2012: *"It's done! The Commission has adopted my proposal for a European law so that women represent 40% of company board members by 2020."* This would be fantastic progress – but let's see where we actually are in 2020.

In the meantime, what is still a fact is that at GCSE and A level stage, girls achieve better grades than boys, and at university nearly 60% of candidates are now female, with a larger percentage of female candidates than male candidates achieving first or upper second class degrees.

I have four children, three girls and one boy, and have watched them develop and grow and have seen them in action through GCSEs, A levels and degrees. I am grateful that all have done very well in their chosen careers, but it was interesting to watch them studying. The girls were much more methodical; they had study timetables with scheduled breaks and treats and their bedroom walls were covered in diagrams. In contrast, I would see my son cramming like crazy the night before a crucial exam. It did him no harm in the end, as he is currently a captain in the Royal Engineers, but I saw a definite difference in approach to studying.

> "Nothing in life comes easy. You have to earn everything. So you have to know the difference between what you want and what you need."
> Sarah Jessica Parker

The international woman director

The proportion of women in senior roles varies dramatically from country to country. Russia has the strongest representation, with 46% of senior roles held by women (this includes senior management roles as well as board positions). Hong Kong has 33%, the US 27% and Australia 24%, while the UK lags behind with 20%. Of economically progressive countries, only India and Japan, with 14% and 15% respectively, are behind the UK.

Looking purely at boardroom positions, in the US just 3% of the Fortune 500 CEOs are women. In the UK, only 10% of the 2,775 directors serving on FTSE 350 company boards are female (and 40% of these companies have all-male boards!). According to the Cranfield report of April 2013, 17% of all board seats in the UK are held by women. In Norway the equivalent figure is 40%, although in the US it is only 16% and in Saudi Arabia only 0.1%.

DOES A DIVERSE BOARD IMPROVE PERFORMANCE?

> "Women invest with their heads, men with testosterone."
> Angela Knight, Chief Executive, Energy UK

Studies carried out by Eversheds, a London-based law firm, and those done by McKinsey, the global consultancy company, found that large European businesses that had at least three women on their management boards significantly out-performed their sector in terms of average return on equity.

But this is not just about female numbers on boards. What is important is the mix on the board as a whole – mixed groups offer better focus than all-male boards, which often have a competitive, "male" way of thinking.

Lehman Brothers failed, and Lehman Sisters might not have done any better, but perhaps Lehman Brothers and Sisters could have weathered the storm.

MY OWN EXPERIENCE

Frankly, in my personal experience, the woman has often fought so hard to get the role that she tends to prepare more conscientiously for meetings and ask the awkward questions more often, so decisions are less likely to be nodded through and so are likely to be better.

I am not alone in thinking that many females are internally programmed to want to impress.

Even as recently as five years ago on an appointment to a new all-male board on a short-term interim role, so anxious was I to impress that I regularly stayed up all night preparing for meetings and trying to identify the key issues in advance of my colleagues. I needed them to know quickly that I could do the job, and this was the only way I knew how.

There are three main areas in which a diverse board can help improve a company's performance.

Improved corporate governance

Following the scandals at several large companies in the late 1990s, the Sarbanes–Oxley Act of 2002 in the US and the Higgs Review of corporate governance in 2003 in the UK called for significant changes to the composition of corporate boards. The Lord Davies report of 2012 has re-emphasised this requirement. But do women really want quotas? I have yet to meet a woman who wants a seat on a board to meet a statistical requirement. Every woman I meet wants to be on the board because she has earned her place.

So there is little appetite for a mandatory quata system, at least in the UK. But what should not be forgotten is that several studies have shown that a mixed board is generally more successful than a single-sex one.

Women consumers

According to *Marketing to Women* by Marti Barletta (Kaplan, 2006), 73% of US household spending decisions are made by women.

Consumer-facing industries already rank among those with the greatest proportion of women on the board. So why are women not fairly represented on the boards of those companies that are promoting the products they buy? It doesn't seem to make sense.

Female attitudes to risk

In research published by Odean and Barber, it was demonstrated that women tended to be much more risk-averse investors than men. This does not mean that women won't take risks, but they may consider matters in a more measured way.

Professor Nick Wilson at Leeds University Business School showed that having at least one female director on the board appears to reduce a company's likelihood of becoming bankrupt by 20% and that having two or three female directors lowered the likelihood of bankruptcy even further. Professor Wilson went on to state that: *"The negative correlation between female directors and insolvency risk appears to hold good."*

BARRIERS TO ACHIEVING DIVERSITY

Of course, achieving diversity has its problems, some of which are described below.

Lack of suitable candidates

I don't believe that there is a lack of suitable candidates, but I do believe that there is a lack of suitable candidates who believe they have the skills to do the job. Men tend to believe they can until proven that they can't. Women believe they can only when they have shown they can. Men ask "*Why can't I do it?*", while women are more likely to say "*I think I can do it.*"

We can debate whether this is the result of nurture or nature, but personal confidence is an important part of success. If you lack confidence, try faking it. The results are amazing: the more you do this, the more real your actual confidence becomes. I speak from vast experience. The more I tell myself I can do it, the more I seem able to achieve whatever "it" is.

Female versus male

There are two particular character traits that are likely to impede professional progress for women.

Confidence

I have always told my children that they can do anything, be anything. I have put them in professional meeting situations from a young age and have proudly taken them to events and encouraged them to network. I have always told them that every setback is a chance to move forward. I have rarely criticised them and have always supported their decisions, even when I have not agreed with them. As a result I have very successful and balanced children. This could be luck, but I know for sure that if you constantly tell someone that they can't achieve, very few will use that to their advantage.

It is a surprise that in the twenty-first century we still have too many people who have not yet accepted that women are more than capable of carrying out the most senior of roles.

Ambition

How often have you heard: "Oh, I can't possibly do that. They wouldn't want me!" Some have called this the sticky floor. For a number of women, their lack of career progression becomes self-perpetuating: "They won't want me, so I won't bother applying." As I have said to my own children and my own staff, you certainly have to be in it to win it!

The work-life balance

For many women, and particularly for those with a caring role, we always seem to be in the wrong place at the wrong time. Our feelings of guilt are simply a way of life as we try to be the perfect wife and mother as well as a successful businesswoman.

I don't think my husband felt the same guilt. Maybe he did – to be honest, we never discussed it in detail – but even now I know that I am generally the one who manages most of the domestic and personal duties alongside my busy work schedule, and I know I am not alone. I understand that my children share the workload in a more balanced way, but domestic arrangements are still heavily geared towards the woman.

If you are male and are now feeling annoyed because this doesn't apply to you, then I would say: "Congratulations! And welcome to our world." As far as I can tell, you are in the minority, but I would love to be proved wrong.

MY OWN EXPERIENCE

I have brought up four children while working all over the world and running numerous businesses. I have not had it all and don't believe it's possible. I have made plenty of sacrifices. Some I chose, some I didn't, but in order to achieve my goal of independence I had to miss numerous school events. I am lucky I never missed a birthday or Christmas but the children were largely brought up by a nanny.

Regrets? No. Regrets are a bit pointless, and anyway they're all grown up now. I believe they would tell you that they missed out on very little, and they're well balanced, happy and successful and I have a wonderful relationship with all of them. I chose – you need to do the same!

The appointment process

If imposing quotas doesn't seem like quite the right route, what could help is a positive approach to the recruitment process. We need some sort of assurance that shortlists are evenly balanced; that female candidates actually get the opportunity to be seen by the interview panel; that we have a 50/50 chance of getting the post. That would be an achievement!

MAKING CHANGES

The UK

In July 2012, as a result of the Davies Report the previous year, the UK Coalition Government Agreement pledged to *"promote gender equality on the boards of listed companies"*.

The Secretary of State for Business, Vince Cable, said in 2012:

> "The progress we have seen in the past year proves that the UK's business-led approach to achieving boardroom diversity is working. The Voluntary Code of Conduct has played a key part in this progress.
>
> "Diverse boards are better boards: benefiting from fresh perspectives, talent, new ideas and broader experience which enable businesses to better reflect and respond to the needs of their customers. This is good for women,

good for companies who need to be the best they can be
in order to compete in today's tough global market
place and ultimately good for the UK economy as a
whole. It is essential that executive search firms and
chairmen continue to use the code to
increase this rate of change."

International changes

In the meantime, many countries in Europe are taking their own
action.

- In **Spain**, a gender equality law was passed in 2007 obliging
  businesses with more than 250 employees to have at least
  40% women on their boards by 2015.
- In **France**, a bill has been passed requiring 40% of board
  members to be women by 2017 for listed businesses and by
  2020 for unlisted businesses.
- In **Italy**, Consob, the Italian Companies and Exchange
  Commission, enforced a resolution requiring that all
  listed companies guarantee a gender balance on their
  boards and announced a system of sanctions that could
  be applied should companies fail to comply with the
  regulations.

Outside Europe, in Canada, Quebec passed legislation in 2006 requiring
gender parity on the boards of its state-owned enterprises, whose
boards comprised just 28% women at the time. The 50% target was
reached in December 2011.

In Australia, reporting guidelines in operation since 2010 require
businesses to disclose the proportion of women on their boards.

And in South Africa there have been calls to introduce a 30% quota.
A bill is yet to be presented but this would give the government the
power to force companies to appoint women to a good number of all
top positions.

THE FUTURE

Unbelievably, as I write this chapter, the Church of England has just voted not to allow women priests to become bishops, with Tom Wright, a former bishop of Durham, stating that so-called "progress" has led to modern ideas such as the gas chambers. We clearly have a long way to go!

My own position, however, is and always has been that self-affirmation and self-esteem will go a long way to helping you achieve success.

Finally, as Albert Einstein reputedly said: *"The definition of insanity is to keep doing the same thing over and over again and expecting different results."*

So be part of the change. Change the status quo. Fight for what's right and what works. Even if you can't do it for yourself, do it for the next generation.

THE END OF THE JOURNEY, THE START OF AN ADVENTURE

Once you have checked out the various guides in the appendices you should be well equipped to start your adventure to secure the boardroom success you deserve. Armed with information about both the positives and negatives of the role, and with access to tips on securing the post, it leaves only the final ingredient to make this a perfect recipe – you!

Although the twenty-first century has brought a worldwide economic crisis not seen before in our lifetimes, such scenarios also bring opportunities for those wise enough to spot them and daring enough to take the risks needed to achieve success.

The aim of this book is to provide you with an understanding of what makes a great director so that you can rise to the challenges and reach your destination, confident that you have given the role your best, behaved properly and supported others on the way, and that you will leave a positive legacy.

Many people strive for success, while others seem to fall into successful positions. Whichever person you are, I hope this book provides you with the focus to hold on to the keys to the boardroom for as long as you want and with the skills to improve the boardroom and all those who sit around the board table with you.

I wish you much luck.

Jo Haigh
June 2013

Quiz

So what do you know about the role of a director?

Choose from the multiple choice answers to each question. There is only one correct legal or governance answer.

1. What is a director?
   a) Someone who is subordinate to the chair.
   b) Someone appointed for her functional expertise.
   c) One among equals in the boardroom.
   d) Someone heading up a functional responsibility.

2. From where does a director's authority come?
   a) The articles of association.
   b) The size of her shareholding.
   c) The amount of responsibility delegated to her by the chair.
   d) Her executive title within the company.

3. Just how much should a director participate in board matters?
   a) She should only do so when asked by the chair.
   b) She should only speak on matters related to her executive responsibilities.
   c) She should speak on all matters but not be critical of executive management.
   d) She should be prepared to offer opinions or advice on all items appearing on the agenda.

4. When is a director responsible for board decisions made when she is not there?
   a) She isn't responsible if her objection is minuted.
   b) She is responsible on all occasions where there is a properly constituted board meeting.
   c) She is not responsible if the meeting was called without reasonable notice.
   d) She would never be held responsible for decisions made in her absence.

5. When is a director free of her liabilities for decisions she took part in?
   a) After she has tendered her resignation.
   b) After the company has gone into liquidation.
   c) After an administrative receiver has been appointed.
   d) Never.

6. Who is responsible for the day-to-day running of a company?
   a) The company secretary.
   b) The heads of management departments.
   c) The managing director.
   d) The chair.

7. Who is responsible for filing the statutory returns?
   a) The company secretary.
   b) The company secretary together with the board.
   c) The board of directors.
   d) The auditors together with the company secretary.

8. Who is responsible for the final wording of the board minutes?
   a) The chair.
   b) The board of directors.
   c) The company secretary.
   d) The company lawyer.

9. How much notice does a board meeting require?
   a) None.
   b) Seven days in writing.

c) It must be announced at the previous meeting.
d) Reasonable time given the circumstances.

10. When does a director have to account to the board for her department?
    a) At every board meeting.
    b) When required by the managing director, as long as she is suitably briefed before the meeting.
    c) Directly through her departmental report.
    d) Never.

11. Who takes responsibility for setting long-term corporate strategy?
    a) The executive directors.
    b) The executive directors plus the senior managers.
    c) The chair, managing director and non-executive directors.
    d) The board of directors.

12. Who is responsible for the chair's decisions?
    a) The chair.
    b) The company.
    c) The board of directors.
    d) All of the above.

13. Who decides on the constitution of the board?
    a) The board as a whole.
    b) The shareholders.
    c) The chair with the assistance of non-executive directors.
    d) The executive directors.

14. Legally, how often must a board meet?
    a) Each month.
    b) Whenever the chair decides to do so.
    c) As stated in the memorandum of association.
    d) Once a year to prepare the directors' report.

15. When is it considered reasonable for a director to miss a board meeting?

a) When she is sick.
b) When she takes her annual holiday.
c) When an important business deal comes up.
d) When it is socially inconvenient to be present.

16. If you are a lone dissenter in a decision, are you still responsible?
    a) Yes, under collective responsibility.
    b) No, you made your position clear.
    c) No, this would be against natural justice.
    d) Probably not if you threatened resignation.

17. When should a director insist on minuting her dissent?
    a) On every disagreement of policy.
    b) On matters of principle.
    c) Whenever she feels she is in the right.
    d) When she is a director of a public company.

18. In a case of suspected insolvency, who is responsible for taking the initial action?
    a) The board of directors.
    b) The finance director.
    c) A partner at the company's auditors.
    d) The chair of a creditors' meeting.

19. To avoid a charge of wrongful trading, whose interests must first be considered?
    a) The company's shareholders.
    b) The company's bank.
    c) The directors.
    d) The company's creditors.

20. Who is responsible if financial accounts are not filed at Companies House on time?
    a) The officers of the company.
    b) The company secretary.
    c) The board of directors.
    d) The chair and company secretary.

21. What is the maximum period for which the courts can disqualify a director?
    a) For 15 years.
    b) For 5 years.
    c) For life, if she is the managing director or finance director.
    d) None, if the individual is a non-executive director.

22. What rights does a 10% share in a company give you?
    a) To bring a derivative action against a director.
    b) To block a sale in a private company.
    c) To pass an ordinary resolution.
    d) To have a seat on the board.

23. To which third party does a director owe her first and primary duty?
    a) The company.
    b) Customers.
    c) Employees.
    d) Creditors.

24. What is the maximum period of a director's service contract before it needs shareholder approval?
    a) 18 months.
    b) 12 months.
    c) 3 years.
    d) 5 years.

25. What sort of offence is an offence under the Health and Safety Act?
    a) A criminal offence.
    b) A civil offence.
    c) Both.
    d) None.

26. Which of these could trigger a director being disqualified?
    a) Conviction of a summary offence.
    b) Fraud when winding up a company.

c) Entering an individual voluntary arrangement (IVA).

d) Becoming an overseas resident.

27. If you act as a director while disqualified, who is liable for the company debts?
    a) The company.
    b) The shareholders.
    c) You and the board.
    d) The bank.

28. How many directors are required for a quorum?
    a) One.
    b) Two.
    c) It depends on the articles of association.
    d) It depends on the memorandum.

The answers are as follows:

1) c
2) a
3) d
4) b
5) d
6) c
7) c
8) b
9) d
10) b
11) d
12) d
13) b
14) d
15) a
16) a
17) b
18) a
19) d
20) c

21) a
22) a
23) a
24) a
25) c
26) c
27) b
28) c

Appendices

Appendices

Appendix 1

Types of company director

A director is defined in the Companies Act 2006 as anyone carrying out that function by whatever name they are called. In fact, it is entirely possible to be a director without knowing you are one and certainly without having the title of "director".

The following are examples of the most common types of director.

EXECUTIVE DIRECTORS

Executive directors have a functional management role alongside their role as a board director and have a specific functional responsibility, such as finance director, sales director or operations director. They are employees as well as board members and have **service contracts** that describe their dual role.

NON-EXECUTIVE DIRECTORS

Non-executive directors are generally not employees and they have no functional or departmental role. They may hold several such roles in a variety of companies. They have a **contract for services** as opposed to a service contract (see above). A contract for services is for an individual who takes a directorship as a self-employed person, so their contract does not cover employment issues.

SHADOW DIRECTORS

A shadow director is defined in the Companies Act as *"a person in accordance with whose directions or instructions the directors of the company are accustomed to act."* It is quite possible that such people sit outside the company, as either advisers or consultants (although, under the Companies Act, lawyers and accountants acting in their professional capacity cannot be shadow directors). These people can, if proven to be shadow directors, have the same liabilities as any other director, regardless of their knowledge or intent.

ALTERNATE DIRECTORS

An alternate director is someone who is sent to carry out the actions of a director, such as attending a board meeting and contributing to a debate. As such, they have exactly the same liabilities as any other director for any activity in which they are engaged. A **proxy**, on the other hand, acts purely on instruction, and has no liability.

ASSOCIATE DIRECTORS

Companies or employees can sometimes choose to use the title "director" without such a position being officially recorded at Companies House. For example, if a head of sales refers to herself as the sales director, then she creates liability for herself and binds the company to any decisions she makes, just as any other director would. The test of whether an individual is an associate director is one of reasonableness.

Appendix 2

Types of business status in the UK

PRIVATE LIMITED COMPANY (LTD)

This is the most common form of company in the UK. This entity needs only one director and one shareholder and, since the Companies Act 2006, no longer needs a company secretary.

Anyone can set up a limited company. You need only £1 of share capital, although most people start with £100. These businesses must file their accounts at Companies House within nine months of their year end.

PUBLIC LIMITED COMPANY (PLC)

To list your business on the full London Stock Exchange, you need a minimum of £750,000 of share capital. In a listed company, anyone with the funds can buy or sell their shares. A PLC must have at least two directors, two shareholders, a company secretary and a trading certificate.

The costs of listing, and indeed maintaining a listing, are substantial – upwards of £1 million per year. As a result, the companies that choose to be listed and remain so tend to be substantial. These companies must file their accounts within six months of their year end and cannot file abbreviated information.

PUBLIC LIMITED COMPANY (PLC): NOT TRADING ON THE STOCK EXCHANGE

Most companies that choose to use the acronym PLC are not in fact listed on any exchange. To all intents and purposes, they are very similar to private limited companies in that they do not trade their shares in the same way as the PLCs mentioned above.

Unlike private limited companies, non-trading PLCs must have at least two directors, two shareholders and a qualified company secretary. They cannot produce abbreviated accounts and must post accounts within six months of their year end. However, they need £50,000 of share capital and only a quarter of this needs to be fully paid up, so technically a PLC could have only £12,500 of capital.

LIMITED LIABILITY PARTNERSHIP (LLP)

Probably the best way to describe an LLP is as a partnership in the traditional sense but wrapped inside a company shell. In a traditional partnership, the partners have unlimited liabilities, there is no need for a written partnership agreement, and there is absolute privacy of information in the public domain.

However, an LLP cannot come into existence without a written partnership agreement. An LLP must produce accounts that are available for public view and must have these audited when the partnership reaches the relevant turnover figure. As a result of this transparency, the members of the partnership are afforded a level of protection similar to that of a shareholder, with a designated member having a similar status to a director. Unlike a company, an LLP is taxed under partnership tax rules rather than company tax rules.

GUARANTEE COMPANY

These companies are often what are termed not-for-profit or third sector businesses. Whereas a company registered with shares makes a dividend distribution to its shareholders, companies limited by guarantee have trustees or guarantors instead of shareholders and no distribution is made to them. However, these companies do have boards of directors who have exactly the same liabilities as directors in a company limited by shares.

UNLIMITED COMPANY

It is possible to register what is called an "unlimited company", although there are not vast numbers of these. These companies look and act exactly like a traditional company, the main difference being that the shareholders have unlimited liability. (In traditional limited companies, shareholders' liabilities are limited to their investment.) Unlimited companies do not have to publish their accounts in the public domain.

SOCIETAS EUROPAEA (SE)

These are companies that can be resident anywhere in Europe but are registered in Brussels and subject to the law of the European Economic Community; there are multiple exceptions to this, including, but not limited to, health and safety law, employment law and taxation. Anyone wanting to set up a company of this type must operate in at least two European Economic Community countries and must have a minimum share capital of the euro equivalent of £50,000.

SOLE TRADER

This is the simplest and most common way to trade. A sole trader is just a single person buying and selling or providing a service in her own name. There are very few requirements when establishing such an enterprise: it requires no registration and no accounts have to be filed, although tax has to be paid as it becomes due. Trading in this manner represents a huge personal risk, as any activity undertaken as a sole trader is the sole and absolute responsibility of the individual.

Appendix 3

The perfect board meeting agenda

A good agenda should provide the stimulus for strategic debate and operational review, and it should prompt the chair and promote decision-making.

The following is a suggested agenda that I have developed over the years and find to be very useful in encouraging good practice.

THE AGENDA

1. Apologies
This is to establish who is present, who isn't, and whether there is a quorum for any matters being discussed.

2. Declaration of any conflict of interest
Directors have a legal duty to avoid conflicts of interest with the company. It is therefore essential that, if they are aware of any discussion due to take place that may cause them a conflict, they must mention it at the start of the meeting so the chair can deal with it appropriately.

3. Any other business (AOB)
Most people think this is the last item on the agenda. However, if it is moved to the start, it gives control of the meeting back to the

chair – the AOB declared may not actually be discussed at this point, but the chair can make a decision on its priority, which stops the grenade-throwing assassin mentioned in Chapter 1.

4. Approval of the minutes of the previous meeting

A call for approval should be prompted and, if passed, the minutes signed by the chair. A copy of the minutes should be retained by the company and copies circulated to the rest of the board.

5. Matters outstanding

Any matters not appearing elsewhere on the agenda should be dealt with here. This section of the board meeting is to ensure that actions carried forward from the last meeting are being addressed.

6. Sign-offs and compliance

This includes those matters that require periodic board sign-off, for example the approval of budgets and capital expenditure.

7. Health and safety

Health and safety is the subject of much litigation and should be of grave importance to directors. It therefore needs priority on the agenda and its own agenda item.

8. Management reports

These are generally produced by executive directors to summarise the activities of their particular department. They are used to inform and educate other fellow directors and allow the whole board to contribute to any issue that they highlight. They should all have been submitted to the board in advance and only be discussed by exception at the meeting.

9. Committee reports

These reports should be dealt with in the same manner as the management reports mentioned above.

10. Risk management

More than ever in the current economic climate, the board must not only evaluate its risks but have in place procedures to minimise and manage any such situations.

11. Environmental management

Green is the new black, with boards having extensive legal and moral duties to manage the company's environmental impact and procedures.

12. Corporate responsibility

Corporate responsibility is no longer something boards can pay lip-service to. It has been embraced by the larger companies for some time and is widely recognised as having a major positive effect on staff recruitment and retention as well as a huge impact on the bottom line.

13. Strategic objectives review

It helps to have identified the half a dozen or so items that are critical to the business achieving its annual plan and targets. These items should be reviewed and analysed, and decisions made on progress or changes required.

14. Policy review

If on average a board meets once a month, taking the opportunity to review and confirm a different policy at each meeting shows good practice and keeps the board up to date on critical procedures.

15. Special agenda items

This covers any matters that are pertinent at a particular time to the business in question. Make sure that you keep these items strategic: this is not the place to discuss why Fred is always late! That's for the management meeting.

16. External presentation

Boards, particularly those that comprise predominantly executive directors, can become very internally focused. They often veer towards management meetings, as the directors may feel more comfortable with this than with a discussion of strategy. The use of a third-party presenter, even if not every month, can stimulate the board to think more widely and deeply and can provide an educational platform to improve board members' skills.

17. Date of the next meeting

Although these should all be tabled 12 months in advance, this is the opportunity to reconfirm the next date.

Appendix 4

Sample board papers

These are the templates I like to use for papers to be presented during a board meeting.

REGULAR BOARD PAPER

Name:

Department:

Period:

Overview of period:

Key issues:

Actions taken:	Advice required:

BOARD PAPER FOR A SPECIFIC REQUIREMENT

Name:

Department:

Date:

Summary of the proposal:
[What it is that the author of the paper is seeking to achieve and why]

Costs and benefits of the proposal:

What are the risks that have been identified by the author and what processes are suggested to manage such risks?

What is the planned implementation timeline and what contingencies have been accounted for?

What, if any, information is still needed before this project can commence? Who is responsible for gathering this and when will it be available?

What does the author of this paper require from the board to proceed and by when?

Further information attached to this paper as needed:

Signed:

Date:

Appendix 5

The appointment process

This appendix contains sample appointment documents that I have found useful (these are for guidance only and are not intended as a substitute for proper legal advice) and some data on directors' remuneration.

SERVICE AGREEMENT FOR AN EXECUTIVE DIRECTOR

You can download a template for a service agreement at www.employmentlawcontracts.co.uk/samples/directorsservicecontract.doc. Or feel free to use or adapt the following template, which I have developed with various companies I have worked for and which covers the main points.

The service agreement

This Agreement is made on [date] of [month] [year]

Between:

(1) [company] **Ltd**, a company registered under the laws of England whose registered office is at [address] (company number [number]) (the **"Company"**); and

(2) [employee] of [address] (the **"Executive"**).

It is hereby agreed as follows:

Definitions and interpretation

In this Agreement the following words and expressions shall, except where the context requires otherwise, have the following meanings:

"Associated Company"   in relation to the Company, another company which is a subsidiary or subsidiary undertaking of, or a holding company or parent undertaking of, or another subsidiary or subsidiary undertaking of a holding company or parent undertaking of, the Company;

"Board"   the Board of Directors from time to time of the Company and any duly appointed Committee of the Board;

"Business"   the carrying on of the business of [*activity of business*] and any and all other business or management services in which the Company or any Associated Company shall be engaged, concerned or interested from time to time and in which the Executive was involved or had contact and dealings during the course of this Agreement;

"Confidential Business Information"   any information of a confidential or secret nature (including without limitation customer accounts, global and regional operations, investment strategies and projects, trade secrets, inventions, designs, formulae, financial information, technical information, marketing information, and lists of customers) whether or not recorded in documentary form or on computer disc or tape;

"Customer"   any person, firm, company or other organisation whatsoever to whom the Company or any Associated Company has supplied Business;

"Employment"	the Executive's employment under this Agreement or, as the context requires, its duration;
"ERA 1996"	Employment Rights Act 1996;
"Gross Misconduct"	includes but is not limited to discrimination, harassment, fighting, alcohol or drug abuse, fraud, competing with the Company, theft, destruction of Company property, any breach of the Company's e-mail/internet policy, serious breaches of health and safety rules and breach of a statute which has a direct effect on the Executive's ability to undertake her duties under this Agreement;
"Group"	the Company and each Associated Company (if any);
"Incapacity"	any illness, accident or other like cause which prevents the Executive from performing her duties hereunder;
"Intellectual Property"	includes, without limitation, copyright material, inventions, designs (whether registrable or not), processes, products, formulae, notations, improvements, know-how, goodwill, reputation, moulds, get-up, logos, devices, plans, models, literary material, computer codes, studies, data, charts, specifications, computer firmware and software, any work consisting of a computer program or work generated by a computer, pre-contractual and contractual documents and all drafts of the above works and materials and working papers relating to such works and materials;
"Intellectual Property Rights"	includes patents, registered and unregistered design rights, trademarks, service marks, trade names, goodwill, copyrights, moral rights, database rights and all other intellectual property rights (in each case in

	any part of the world and whether or not registered or registrable and to the fullest extent thereof and for the full period thereof and all extensions and renewals thereof) and all applications for registration thereof;
"Production"	(and consonant expressions) used in relation to Relevant Intellectual Property includes the invention, creation, conception, improvement, discovery, design, research, development and manufacture thereof;
"Recognised Investment Exchange"	any body of persons which is for the time being a Recognised Investment Exchange for the purposes of the Financial Services and Markets Act 2000;
"The Regulations"	Working Time Regulations 1998;
"Relevant Intellectual Property"	all Intellectual Property produced invented, created, conceived or discovered by the Executive either alone or with any other person at any time now or hereafter during the continuance in force of this Agreement (whether or not in the course of her employment hereunder) which is Intellectual Property of the kind produced at any such time by the Company or any Associated Company, or relates directly or indirectly to the Business or which may in the reasonable opinion of the Company be capable of being used or adapted for use therein or in connection therewith;
"Restricted Territory"	any area or country in which the Company or Associated Company shall carry on Business;
"Subsidiary", **"Subsidiary Undertaking"**, **"Holding Company"** and **"Parent Undertaking"**	the meanings respectively ascribed thereto by sections 736 and 736A of the Companies Act 1985 (as amended).

References in this Agreement and in any schedules to statutes shall include any statute modifying, re-enacting, extending or made pursuant to the same or which is modified, re-enacted, or extended by the same.

Headings are for ease of reference only and shall not be taken into account in the construction of this Agreement.

Any reference to the Executive shall, if appropriate, include her personal representatives.

Any reference in this Agreement to a clause or sub-clause is to the relevant clause or sub-clause of this Agreement.

Any schedules to this Agreement form an integral part thereof and any reference to this Agreement includes a reference to such schedules.

Nothing in this Agreement shall prohibit the Executive from making a protected disclosure under the Public Interest Disclosure Act 1998.

Statutory particulars of employment

This Agreement contains the statutory particulars of employment required by section 1 of the ERA 1996. There are no collective agreements in force which directly affect the terms and conditions of the Executive's employment.

Appointment

The Company appoints the Executive as [*title*] director, or in such other capacity.

Place of work

The Executive will work at the Company's offices at [*address*] on a regular basis or such other location as the Company may require from time to time.

Term

The Executive's employment shall start on the Commencement Date and shall continue thereafter unless and until terminated by either party, giving to the other not less than **three months'** prior notice.

No employment with a previous employer will count as part of the Executive's period of continuous employment with the Company.

The Company shall be entitled to pay salary in lieu of notice in any case where it might otherwise serve notice for any reason to terminate the Executive's employment.

Powers, duties and working hours
During the continuance of the Executive's employment the Executive shall:

- Be flexible in her approach to work because of the nature of the Company's business demands. The Executive shall carry out such duties and exercise such powers to manage and promote the interests of the Business of the Company or Group as may from time to time be vested, authorised, and delegated to her and at such place as determined by the Company;
- Devote all of her working time, attention and abilities to carrying out her duties hereunder and give the full benefit of her knowledge and skill to the Company and any Associated Company;
- Carry out her duties in a proper, diligent, faithful and efficient manner and use her best endeavours to promote and maintain the interests and reputation of the Group;
- Comply with all reasonable directions given to her by the Board and keep the Board promptly and fully informed (in writing as required) of the conduct of the Business or affairs of the Group and provide such explanations and information as the Board may require in connection with such Business or affairs;
- At all times comply with all rules and regulations of the Company which are consistent with this Agreement;
- Refrain from making false or misleading statements about the Group;
- Work the Company's normal working hours which are [hours] on [days of the week] and such additional hours as may be necessary or appropriate from time to time in order for the

Executive properly and effectively to carry out her duties. Both parties agree that the Executive's working time is not measured or predetermined or capable of being determined in accordance with Regulation 20 of the Regulations.

The Company may from time to time appoint any other person to act on the Executive's behalf in the event that the Executive cannot perform her duties under this Agreement due to Incapacity.

Working Time Regulations

It is assumed that the Executive does not fall within one of the exceptions to Part III of the Regulations, in particular Regulation 20, which applies where the Executives of the Company and the Executive agree that the limit in Regulation 4(1) (the maximum average 48-hour weekly working time) of the Regulations shall not apply to the Executive's employment. The agreement under this clause will remain in force until the termination of this Agreement. The Executive may terminate any agreement under this clause at any time by giving not less than three months' written notice to the Company.

Remuneration

The Executive shall be paid a basic salary at the initial rate of £[*amount*] per annum (inclusive of any Director's fees payable as Director of the Company or any Associated Company) which shall be reviewed from time to time but without commitment to increase.

Such salary shall accrue from day to day and will be subject to income tax and national insurance deductions and will be paid directly into the Executive's bank account by equal monthly instalments in arrears on or about the last day of each month.

The Executive will be entitled to participate in a Company discretionary bonus scheme. [*Brief detail of scheme*] The bonus is paid at the absolute discretion of the Board.

Expenses

The Company shall reimburse to the Executive all reasonable travelling, hotel, telephone and other out-of-pocket expenses properly incurred by her in the proper performance of her duties subject to the production of monthly statements of such expenses including, where relevant, the appropriate VAT invoices and such other evidence as the Company may require.

The Company will not be providing a company car but will pay for the Executive's reasonable business mileage costs at the prevailing rate for the Company (if any) or the United Kingdom provided the Executive complies with the company procedures.

Deductions

The Company reserves the right to deduct from the Executive's salary, bonus or any payments due to the Executive on the termination of this Agreement or any other sums due to the Executive any sums which the Executive may owe the Company including any overpayments or loans made to the Executive by the Company or losses suffered by the Company as a result of the Executive's negligence or breach of Company rules.

Pension and benefits

The Company offers access to a contributory pension scheme (the **"Scheme"**) and will match the Executive's contribution up to 5% of the Executive's basic salary into the Scheme. Further details of the Scheme are available from the Company. There is no contracting out certificate in force in respect of the Executive's employment.

During the continuance of this Agreement the Executive will also be entitled to participate at the Company's expense in the Company's Life Assurance scheme with [*insurer*] which provides for four times salary on death in service subject to the rules of that scheme from time to time in force.

Holidays

The Company's holiday year runs from [*date*] to [*date*] (the **"Holiday Year"**). In addition to public and bank holidays the Executive shall be entitled in every Holiday Year to 20 working days' paid holiday. The Executive shall not be entitled to carry forward any unused part of her holiday to the next Holiday Year, which holiday entitlement shall be lost.

For the Holiday Year during which the Executive's employment commences or terminates the Executive's holiday entitlement shall accrue on a pro rata basis proportional to the number of days worked during that Holiday Year. On the termination of the Executive's employment, the Executive shall be entitled to pay in lieu of outstanding holiday and shall be required to repay to the Company holiday taken in excess of the Executive's entitlement.

Holiday pay shall be calculated in accordance with the Executive's basic salary.

The Company may require the Executive to take all or any part of any outstanding holiday during any period of notice.

Incapacity

If the Executive is absent from work due to Incapacity she shall notify the Company as soon as possible about the nature of her illness and how long she is likely to be absent. If the incapacity continues for seven or more consecutive days the Executive shall provide a medical practitioner's statement on the eighth day and weekly thereafter. Immediately following the Executive's return to work after a period of absence the Executive shall complete a self-certification form which shall be made available by the Company.

If the Executive is absent from work due to Incapacity (but excluding any illness or accident caused by the Executive's own negligence or self-infliction such as alcoholism and/or drug abuse) duly notified and certified in accordance with Company procedures the Company shall pay the Executive her full remuneration for up to an aggregate of 39 working days absence in any period of 12 months and thereafter such remuneration (if any) as the Board shall in its discretion approve.

If the incapacity shall be occasioned by a third party in respect of which damages are recoverable the Executive shall immediately notify the Board of that fact and of any settlement or judgement made in connection with it and shall give to the Board such particulars and all payments made to the Executive by the Company by way of salary (including any bonus or commission) or sick pay shall to the extent that damages for loss of earnings are recoverable from that third party constitute loans from the Company to the Executive (notwithstanding that as an interim measure income tax and national insurance has been deducted from payments as if they were emoluments of employment) and shall be repaid to the Company when and to the extent that the Executive recovers damages for loss of earnings.

The remuneration paid as detailed shall include any statutory sick pay payable and when this is exhausted shall be reduced by the amount of any state benefits (including state sickness benefit and invalidity benefit) and other benefits recoverable by the Executive (whether or not recovered).

The Company may at its expense at any time whether or not the Executive is then incapacitated require the Executive to submit to such medical examinations and tests by a registered medical practitioner/ consultant nominated by the Company and the Executive hereby authorises such practitioner/consultant to disclose to and discuss with the Company the results of such examinations and tests.

Data protection

The Company may hold and process certain personal data about the Executive for a number of purposes connected with her employment, for example payroll operations and the administration of employee benefits. Processing of personal data by the Company shall be carried out in accordance with the Data Protection Act 1998. The Executive hereby consents to personal data held about her by the Company being processed by the Company as above which may include information being transmitted outside the European Economic Area.

Confidential information

The Executive acknowledges that:

- The Company and any Associated Company possesses a valuable body of Confidential Business Information;
- The Company and any Associated Company will give the Executive access to Confidential Business Information in order that the Executive may carry out her duties;

- Either during the course of the Executive's employment or on leaving the employment of the Company, if the Executive were to disclose any Confidential Business Information to an actual or potential competitor of the Company or any Associated Company or any third party, it would cause a serious competitive disadvantage and immeasurable financial and other damage to the Company or any Associated Company.

The Executive shall during the continuance of her employment and at all times thereafter keep with inviolable secrecy and shall not reveal, make use of, disclose or publish to any person other than the Board or persons nominated by them or otherwise utilise other than for the proper performance of the Executive's duties any Confidential Business Information concerning the affairs or business or products of the Company or of any Associated Company or of any of their predecessors in business or of their suppliers, agents, distributors or Customers of which the Executive may now know or have learned or which the Executive may hereafter know or learn while in the Company's employment.

Intellectual property

All Relevant Intellectual Property and all Intellectual Property Rights therein shall to the fullest extent permitted by law and statute belong to, vest in and be the absolute, sole and unencumbered property of the Company or an Associated Company immediately on its coming into existence and the Company or any Associated Company shall be entitled, free of charge, to the exclusive use thereof.

The Executive hereby:

- Acknowledges for the purposes of section 39 of the Patents Act 1977 that because of the nature of her duties and the particular responsibilities arising from the nature of her duties she has and at all times during her employment will have a special obligation to further the interests of the Business and undertakings of the Company and of any Associated Company;

- Undertakes to notify and disclose to the Company in writing all Relevant Intellectual Property forthwith upon the production of the same and to keep secret and confidential (before or after termination of the Executive's employment) such Relevant Intellectual Property, and promptly whenever requested by the Company and in any event upon the termination of her employment deliver up to the Company all correspondence and other documents, papers and records, and all copies thereof in her possession, custody and power relating to any Relevant Intellectual Property and the Executive shall sign a declaration of compliance that states she undertakes to hold upon trust for the benefit of the Company or any Associated Company any Relevant Intellectual Property and the Intellectual Property Rights therein to the extent the same may not be and until the same are vested absolutely in the Company or any Associated Company;
- Assigns by way of future assignment all copyright, design rights and other propriety rights (if any) in all Relevant Intellectual Property;
- Pursuant to section 77 and the provisions of Chapter IV of Part 1 of the Copyright, Designs and Patents Act 1988, unconditionally and irrevocably waives her rights to be identified as the author of any of the Relevant Intellectual Property in which copyright subsists (**"the Work"**) including any moral rights to the Work and not to have the Work subjected to derogatory treatment; and this waiver is made expressly in favour of the Company and shall extend to licensees and successors in title to the copyright in the Work;
- Acknowledges that, save as provided by law, no further remuneration or compensation other than that provided for herein is or may become due to her in respect of the performance of her obligations under this clause she undertakes at the expense of the Company to execute all such documents and give such assistance as may be necessary or desirable to vest in and register or obtain letters or patents in the name of the Company or any Associated Company and otherwise to protect and maintain the Relevant Intellectual Property and the Intellectual Property Rights therein; and

- Agrees that the Company may, on her behalf, do all such things to vest full right and title to any Relevant Intellectual Property in the Company or as it shall direct and, as regards any third party, the Executive agrees that any such document or act shall be conclusive and binding upon the third party.

The Executive agrees and understands that rights and obligations under this clause apply both during the Executive's employment with the Company and after its termination for whatever reason and shall be binding upon the Executive's representatives.

To the extent that by law any Relevant Intellectual Property or the Intellectual Property Rights therein do not, or are not permitted to, vest in or belong to the Company or any Associated Company the Executive agrees immediately upon the same coming into existence to offer to the Company or any Associated Company in writing a right of first refusal to acquire the same on arm's-length terms to be negotiated and agreed between the parties in good faith.

Restrictions during employment

The Executive shall not during the continuance of her employment without the prior consent in writing of the Board either alone or jointly with or on behalf of others and whether directly or indirectly and whether as principal, partner, agent, shareholder, director, employee, investor or otherwise howsoever engage in, carry on or be interested or concerned in any business other than the Business of the Company or any Associated Company **provided that** nothing in this clause shall preclude the Executive from:

- Holding shares or other securities as a bona fide investment only in any company where such shares or other securities are quoted or otherwise dealt in on a Recognised Investment Exchange and the Executive's aggregate holding of such shares or securities does not constitute more than five per cent of all the equity shares in the capital of that company or confer the right to cast more than five per cent of all the votes ordinarily capable of being cast at general meetings of the shareholders of that company; or

- Maintaining the Executive's present outside business interests and investments as disclosed to, and approved by, the Board **provided always** that;
  - Such business is not at any time in competition with the Company or any Associated Company. The Executive confirms any interests she has are listed in the Schedule attached to this agreement; and
  - The Executive's duties hereunder to the Company shall have priority and that such outside interests shall not unduly interfere with the due and proper performance of such duties.

Share dealings

The Executive shall comply where relevant with every rule of law, every regulation of the UK Listing Authority and/or London Stock Exchange plc or any other market on which the Executive deals and every regulation of the Company in force in relation to dealings in shares, debentures or other securities of the Company or any Associated Company and unpublished price-sensitive information affecting the shares, debentures or other securities of any other company, provided always that in relation to overseas dealings the Executive shall also comply with all laws of the state and all regulations of the stock exchange, market or dealing system in which such dealings take place.

Termination

If the Executive:

- Shall commit any act of dishonesty whether relating to the Company, any Associated Company, an employee or otherwise relating to the Company Business; or
- Is guilty of any Gross Misconduct or commits any serious breach of any of her obligations to the Company or any Associated Company or refuses or neglects to comply with lawful orders given to the Executive by the Board; or
- Is guilty of any conduct which in the reasonable opinion of the Company brings the Executive, the Company or any Associated Company into disrepute; or
- Shall be prohibited or disqualified by law from holding the office which the Executive holds in the Company or any

Associated Company or shall resign from any such office
without the prior written consent of the Board; or

- Is in the reasonable opinion of the Company incompetent in
  the performance of her duties; or
- Fails to observe and perform in all material respects the terms
  and provisions of this Agreement and fails to remedy any
  such non-observance or non-performance (where capable of
  remedy) within fourteen days after prior written notice from
  the Company requiring her so to do; or
- Is declared bankrupt or enters into any composition or
  arrangement with or for the benefit of her creditors including
  a voluntary arrangement under the Insolvency Act 1986; or
- Is convicted of any arrestable criminal offence (other than
  an offence under road traffic or environmental legislation
  for which the Executive is not sentenced to any term of
  imprisonment whether immediate or suspended); or
- Shall be or become of unsound mind or be or become a
  patient under the Mental Health Act 1983; or
- Is prevented from performing her duties due to Incapacity
  (including any illness caused by the Executive's own
  negligence) for a period of 90 working days in aggregate in
  any period of 12 months;

Then the Company shall be entitled at its absolute discretion to
terminate the Executive's employment immediately without notice
or payment in lieu of notice whereupon the Executive shall have no
claim against the Company for damages or otherwise by reason only
of such termination. Further, it is hereby agreed that the Company shall
be entitled to terminate the Executive's employment notwithstanding
that to do so would disentitle the Executive to any benefits under
a permanent health insurance scheme in force at the date of such
termination.

Upon the termination of the Executive's employment for whatever
reason the Executive agrees that:

- In the event that the Executive is required to serve her period
  of notice the Board may in its absolute discretion require

the Executive to perform only such duties as it may allocate to her or not to perform any of her duties or to exclude her from any premises of the Group (without providing any reason therefore) and that the Board may require the Executive to stay away from and have no contact with any employees, officers, customers, clients, agents, trade connections or suppliers of the Group provided always that the Executive's salary and all other contractual benefits shall continue to be paid and provided to the Executive until her employment is terminated; and

- At the request of the Company, immediately resign (without claim for compensation) from all directorships and other offices which she may hold in the Company or in any Associated Company; and
- At the request of the Company, and if applicable, transfer without payment any qualifying or nominee shares held by the Executive to the Company and/or any Associated Company; and in the event of the Executive's failure to do so within seven days of such request the Company may effect such transfers on the Executive's behalf; and
- At the request of the Company, immediately deliver to the Company all Relevant Intellectual Property, Confidential Business Information, documents (including copies), keys, credit cards and other property of the Company or any Associated Company in the Executive's possession including being accompanied by such persons as directed by the Company to such other place in order to retrieve such property.

If notice is not received by the Company within seven days of a request by the Company the Executive hereby irrevocably authorises the Company to appoint a person to execute any documents and to do everything necessary to effect such resignation on the Executive's behalf.

The termination of the Executive's employment for whatever reason shall not affect those provisions of this Agreement which are expressed to have effect thereafter.

The Company may suspend the Executive, on full pay, for the purpose of investigating any misconduct alleged against the Executive and during any such period the Executive shall not, except with the prior consent in writing of the Board, attend at any premises of the Company or any Associated Company or contact any employee, customer or supplier of the Company or any Associated Company. The Company shall be under no obligation to provide any work for the Executive during such period and the Executive shall, at the request of the Company, immediately deliver to the Company all or any of its property.

It is acknowledged that the Executive may, during her employment, be granted rights upon the terms and subject to the conditions of the rules from time to time of a share option scheme or agreement or any other profit-sharing scheme with respect to shares in the Company or any Associated Company. If, on termination of the Executive's employment, whether lawfully or unlawfully, the Executive loses any rights or benefits under such scheme she shall not be entitled to compensation for the loss of any rights under any such scheme.

Directorships

The removal of or failure to re-elect the Executive from or to the office of director of the Company and/or any Associated Company, or if under the Articles of Association for the time being of the Company or of any Associated Company the Executive shall be obliged to retire by rotation, shall not be deemed to be a breach by the Company of this Agreement and the terms hereunder shall continue to apply to her term of employment.

Post-termination obligations

The Executive undertakes to and covenants with the Company that:

- The Executive shall not for a period of 12 months after termination of this Agreement directly or indirectly and in any capacity deal with or engage in business with or be in any way interested in or connected with any person, concern, undertaking, firm or body corporate which engages in or carries on any business within any part of the Restricted Territory in competition with the Business as carried on at the date of termination by the Company or any Associated

Company and where the Executive would be involved in such competing business in the Restricted Territory; and

- The Executive shall not for a period of 12 months after the termination of this Agreement directly or indirectly and in any capacity in competition with the Company or any Associated Company:

  - solicit the custom of, deal with, or provide goods or services of a like description to the Business to any person, firm or company who is or was at any time during the period of 12 months prior to the termination of this Agreement a Customer or client of the Company or any Associated Company (whether or not introduced by the Executive) and with whom the Executive had contact or dealings or other involvement on behalf of the Company or any Associated Company during such 12-month period;

  - canvass, solicit or approach or cause to be canvassed, solicited or approached any person, firm or company who was negotiating with the Company or any Associated Company with a view to becoming a client, supplier or trade connection of the Company in connection with the Business of the Company during the period of 12 months prior to termination of this Agreement and where the Executive was involved in such negotiations or had knowledge of the same during such 12-month period;

  - solicit, interfere with or endeavour to entice away from the Company or any Associated Company any person who is or was employed in a senior capacity or as key personnel or in a sales capacity or director of the Company or any Associated Company (whether or not such person would commit a breach of the terms of her contract of employment by leaving the service of the Company concerned) and with whom the Executive had contact or dealings at any time during the period of 12 months prior to termination of this Agreement or knowingly employ, contract with or assist in or procure the employment or services by any other person, firm or company of any such person; and

- The Executive shall not at any time before or after termination of this Agreement interfere with the relations between the Company or any Associated Company and any of its trade connections or suppliers or entice away such trade connections or suppliers; and
- The Executive shall not at any time before or after the termination of this Agreement, induce or seek to induce by any means involving the disclosure or use of Confidential Business Information any Customer or client, trade connection or supplier to cease dealing with the Company or any Associated Company or to restrict or vary the terms upon which it deals with the Company or any Associated Company; and
- The Executive shall not without the prior authority of the Company remove from the Company's premises, copy or allow others to copy the contents of any document, computer disc, tape or other tangible item which contains any Confidential Business Information or which belongs to the Company.

Each of the obligations on the Executive constitutes a separate and independent restriction on the Executive notwithstanding that it may be contained in the same sub-clause, paragraph, sentence or phrase.

If any obligation set out in this clause or any part thereof shall be held invalid or unenforceable or void but would not be if some part of it were deleted or modified or varied then such provision shall apply with such deletion, modification or variation as may be necessary to make it valid and effective.

The Executive agrees that she shall draw the provisions of this clause to the attention of any third party who may at any time before or after the termination of the Agreement offer to engage the Executive in any capacity and for whom or with whom the Executive intends to work during the period the covenants in this clause are in force.

Disciplinary rules and procedures

The Company does not have any disciplinary rules applicable to the Executive. The Executive shall be expected to exhibit a high standard of propriety in all her dealings with and on behalf of the Company.

Grievance procedure

If the Executive wishes to seek redress of any grievance relating to her employment (other than one relating to a disciplinary decision) the Executive should refer such grievance in writing to the Company chair in the first instance. If the matter is not then settled the Executive should write to the chair of the Group setting out full details of the matter. The Executive must then answer promptly (in writing if so required) such questions (if any) as the chair of the Group wishes to put to the Executive on the matter before she comes to a decision. The decision of the chair of the Group on such matter shall be final.

Email/internet policy

The Executive shall not send any emails of a defamatory, discriminatory or an abusive nature and shall be prohibited from accessing or downloading any pornographic or other offensive material and the Executive will indemnify the Company during and after her employment against all liability resulting from the Executive's breach of this clause. The Company reserves the right to monitor all email/internet activity by the Executive and the Executive acknowledge that such a right falls within the exception set out in Article 8(2) of the European Convention on Human Rights. A breach of this clause is Gross Misconduct and may result in the termination of the Executive's employment.

General

This Agreement supersedes all other agreements whether written or oral between the Company or any Associated Company and the Executive relating to the employment of the Executive including entitlements to equity, share options, shares and bonuses and the Executive agrees that she is not entering into this Agreement in reliance on any representation not expressly set out herein.

The Executive warrants that by virtue of entering into this Agreement she will not be in breach of any express or implied terms of any contract with, or of any other obligation to, any third party binding upon the Executive.

If the employment of the Executive under this Agreement is terminated by reason of the liquidation of the Company for the purpose of reconstruction or amalgamation and the Executive is offered employment with any concern or undertaking resulting from the reconstruction or amalgamation on terms and conditions not less favourable than the terms of this Agreement then the Executive shall be obliged to accept such offer save for any statutory rights the Executive may have, and the Executive shall have no claim against the Company in respect of the termination of her employment.

If any provision of this Agreement shall be unenforceable for any reason but would be enforceable if part of it were deleted, then it shall apply with such deletions as may be necessary to make it enforceable.

Notices

Any notice or other communication given or made under this Agreement shall be in writing and delivered to the relevant party or sent by first class post to the address of that party specified in this Agreement or such other address in England as may be notified by that party from time to time for this purpose, and shall be effectual notwithstanding any change of address not so notified.

Unless the contrary shall be proved, each such notice or communication shall be deemed to have been given or made, if by first class prepaid post, 48 hours after posting and, if by delivery, at the time of delivery.

Changes to terms of employment

The Company reserves the right to make reasonable changes to any of the Executive's terms and conditions of employment with the Executive's consent or by notice.

The Executive shall be notified in writing about any changes under this clause.

Governing law

This Agreement shall be governed by and construed in all respects in accordance with English law and the parties agree to submit to the exclusive jurisdiction of the English Courts or English Employment Tribunals as regards any claim or dispute arising in respect of this Agreement.

Signed by:
[company] Limited
Acting by:

Director
Signed and delivered as a deed by:

[employee]
In the presence of:

SAMPLE LETTER OF APPOINTMENT FOR A NON-EXECUTIVE DIRECTOR

This is taken from the Higgs Report on corporate governance commissioned by the UK government in January 2003 and licensed under the Open Government Licence v1.0. The full report can be read online at www.berr.gov.uk/files/file23012.pdf.

The letter of appointment

On [date], upon the recommendation of the nomination committee, the board of [company] has appointed you as non-executive director. I am writing to set out the terms of your appointment. It is agreed that this is a contract for services and is not a contract of employment.

Appointment

Your appointment will be for an initial term of three years commencing on [date] unless otherwise terminated earlier by and at the discretion of either party upon [one month's] written notice. Continuation of your contract of appointment is contingent on satisfactory performance and re-election at forthcoming AGMs. Non-executive directors are typically expected to serve two three-year terms, although the board may invite you to serve an additional period.

Time commitment

Overall we anticipate a time commitment of [*number of days*] per month after the induction phase. This will include attendance at [*monthly*] board meetings, the AGM, [*one*] annual board away day and [*at least one*] site visit per year. In addition, you will be expected to devote appropriate preparation time ahead of each meeting.

By accepting this appointment, you have confirmed that you are able to allocate sufficient time to meet the expectations of your role. The agreement of the chair should be sought before accepting additional commitments that might impact on the time you are able to devote to your role as a non-executive director of the company.

Role

Non-executive directors have the same general legal responsibilities to the company as any other director. The board as a whole is collectively responsible for the success of the company. The board:

- provides entrepreneurial leadership of the company within a framework of prudent and effective controls which enable risk to be assessed and managed;
- sets the company's strategic aims, ensures that the necessary financial and human resources are in place for the company to meet its objectives, and reviews management performance; and
- sets the company's values and standards and ensures that its obligations to its shareholders and others are understood and met.

All directors must take decisions objectively in the interests of the company.

In addition to these requirements of all directors, the role of the non-executive director has the following key elements:

- **Strategy:** Non-executive directors should constructively challenge and help develop proposals on strategy;

- **Performance:** Non-executive directors should scrutinise the performance of management in meeting agreed goals and objectives and monitor the reporting of performance;
- **Risk:** Non-executive directors should satisfy themselves on the integrity of financial information and that financial controls and systems of risk management are robust and defensible; and
- **People:** Non-executive directors are responsible for determining appropriate levels of remuneration of executive directors and have a prime role in appointing and where necessary removing executive directors in succession planning.

Fees

You will be paid a fee of £[amount] gross per annum which will be paid monthly in arrears, [plus [number] ordinary shares of the company per annum, both of] which will be subject to an annual review by the board. The company will reimburse you for all reasonable and properly documented expenses you incur in performing the duties of your office.

Outside interests

It is accepted and acknowledged that you have business interests other than those of the company and have declared any conflicts that are apparent at present. In the event that you become aware of any potential conflicts of interest, these should be disclosed to the chair and company secretary as soon as apparent.

Confidentiality

All information acquired during your appointment is confidential to the company and should not be released, either during your appointment or following termination (by whatever means), to third parties without prior clearance from the chair.

Your attention is also drawn to the requirements under both legislation and regulation as to the disclosure of price-sensitive information. Consequently you should avoid making any statements that might risk a breach of these requirements without prior clearance from the chair or company secretary.

Induction

Immediately after appointment, the company will provide a comprehensive, formal and tailored induction. We will arrange for site visits and meetings with senior and middle management and the company's auditors. We will also offer to major shareholders the opportunity to meet you.

Review process

The performance of individual directors and the whole board and its committees is evaluated annually. If, in the interim, there are any matters that cause you concern about your role you should discuss them with the chair as soon as is appropriate.

Insurance

The company has directors' and officers' liability insurance and it is intended to maintain such cover for the full term of your appointment. The current indemnity limit is £[*amount*]; a copy of the policy document is attached.

Independent professional advice

Occasions may arise when you consider that you need professional advice in the furtherance of your duties as a director. Circumstances may occur when it will be appropriate for you to seek advice from independent advisers at the company's expense. A copy of the board's agreed procedure under which directors may obtain such independent advice is attached. The company will reimburse the full cost of expenditure incurred in accordance with the attached policy.

Committees

This letter refers to your appointment as a non-executive director of the company. In the event that you are also asked to serve on one or more of the board committees, this will be covered in a separate communication setting out the committee(s)'s terms of reference, any specific responsibilities and any additional fees that may be involved.

EXECUTIVE AND NON-EXECUTIVE DIRECTOR PACKAGES

Executive remuneration packages

Emoluments for directors can be complex, often consisting of an agreed salary plus various benefits such as a car, healthcare, performance bonuses and shares or share options.

In my experience, the average salary for an MD of a small company is probably around £80,000, while other directors earn approximately £60,000. In a larger business these figures could be three and even four times higher. The lowest-paid MDs are in the voluntary sector, with the highest-paid in the financial and accounting sectors, and there still seems to be a north–south divide with regard to pay levels.

Most MDs in small companies (and always when they are shareholders) take a substantial proportion of their income by way of dividends and bonuses. Not only is this tax effective but they can tweak payments to match company needs. Company cars are less attractive now than in the past, as they are only tax efficient for those covering a large number of business miles each year, so most directors opt for a car allowance and a fuel allowance.

The pension opportunities offered in the public sector are rarely available in private companies.

Factors influencing executive pay

Various factors can influence directors' pay and benefits, including other board members, shareholders' expectations, employees' average pay, business regulations, the size and location of the organisation, the business sector in which the company operates, and, of course, the success, strategy and general principles of the business.

Without a doubt the economic crisis has affected pay levels, despite the large salaries and bonuses still paid in the City and reported in the press. Certainly, most directors' fees have at best been frozen for some time and more and more of my clients are moving towards an emphasis on performance-related pay.

Non-executive directors' remuneration

Fees vary hugely for these posts and many people provide these services on a voluntary, unpaid basis.

According to recent research by First Flight, chairs in AIM-listed companies can expect to earn about £40,000 to £50,000 per year for an average of three to four days a month. A non-executive director in the same business will earn approximately half that rate. Some directors charge a flat monthly fee and others a day rate of between £1,500 and £2,000. These rates can fluctuate further if the directors are involved in committee work.

First Flight also found that pay levels were more often related to the size of the organisation than to its financial performance.

Appendix 6

New director checklist

When you are in the process of accepting and commencing a new post, the better informed you are the quicker you will be effective. There is nothing like walking around and talking to people as soon as possible, but having a checklist to make sure you secure the relevant information will help. The following is not an exhaustive list but it is certainly a very comprehensive start.

THE ROLE OF THE DIRECTOR

- What is your role and what strategic objectives have you been given?
- How will you work and with whom?
- Have you seen and are you covered by directors' and officers' liability insurance?
- Have you got copies of all the critical company policies?
- What is the director development process and system of appraisal?
- When are the board meetings and do you have a schedule?
- Is there a board paper format?
- What are the timings for information to be circulated?
- Are you to sit on any board committees? If so, which ones, and what is their composition and brief?

THE OPERATION OF THE BOARD

You need to see:

- CVs and profiles of all the board members
- details of the board structure and roles
- copies of the last six months' board minutes
- the reserved powers list
- the shareholders' agreement
- the agenda for the next meeting
- copies of the last six months' board papers.

THE NATURE OF THE COMPANY, ITS BUSINESS AND ITS MARKETS

Key information here includes:

- a company history, with a summary of significant events
- a summary of products and services
- details of international operations
- the strategy or business plan
- key performance indicators
- the risk register
- up-to-date financial information, including but not limited to management accounts and budgets and the last three years' financial statements
- pension fund details
- insurance and other important policies
- brand management guidelines and the PR and marketing protocol
- details of any major litigation, either current or potential.

CURRENT ISSUES

You should make sure you look at:

- major issues the board and the company are currently focusing on

- remuneration policies and procedures for employees and board members
- AGM and EGM minutes
- the most recent board evaluation report.

SHARES AND SHAREHOLDERS

You need to be aware of:

- policies on directors' share ownership and share dealings
- share schemes and options.

Appendix 7

Insurance policy checklist

When reviewing a company's directors' and officers' liability insurance policy, check the following.

- Does the term "directors and officers" include all directors, including shadow directors?
- Is run-off cover available?
- What is the definition of a claim? Does it cover criminal and civil claims? Are there any exclusions and, if so, are you happy with this?
- Does it cover global operations and related claims if needed?
- What will the policy actually pay for? Does it cover defence costs and prosecution costs?
- How do you have to make a claim? Are there any time restrictions or any exclusions?

As a minimum, the insurance should cover legal costs, damages, charges, expenses and judgments, irrespective of the jurisdiction of the area in which the liability arises.

Appendix 7

Insurance policy checklist

Appendix 8

Sample evaluation questions

As mentioned in the body of the book, I have some concerns about the effectiveness of a "tick box", self-completed board evaluation, but nevertheless they are widely used. My advice is to complement this with a facilitator or observer and some personal one-to-one interviews to really get to grips with serious issues.

The table below lists only some of the questions that could be considered. It is not a complete list and should be used only as a guide.

		RATING			
		Excellent	**Good**	**Fair**	**Poor**
Leadership					
1.	Goals and visions are clearly understood by the board and by me.				
2.	The chair facilitates the meetings well and brings the board to agreement on key issues in a timely manner.				
3.	The board and the company have a good reputation in the local community.				

Planning					
1.	The board has a good and well-communicated business strategy.				
2.	I am satisfied with the personal contribution I am making to the board's strategic planning process.				
3.	The board has appropriate risk management policies and procedures in place.				
4.	The board has a crisis management plan in place.				
Accountability and results					
1.	The board focuses on strategy and not detail.				
2.	The board does not interfere with but supports management.				
3.	I am happy that the board has the correct key performance indicators in place.				
Finance, audit, information and analysis					
1.	The board has appropriate and timely information to hand.				
2.	The board has meetings that are of appropriate duration.				
Board roles and orientation					
1.	The board induction programme is well organised.				
2.	Board meetings are well run.				
Open-ended questions					
1.	I think that we as a board perform well in the following areas:				
2.	I think that we as a board can improve in the following areas:				

Appendix 9

Mentoring and director support organisations

There are numerous groups or one-to-one support organisations for directors; the following represents a small sample.

I am personally aware of all these businesses as both a customer and a supplier. All have first-class reputations and, more importantly, they deliver what they promise. They haven't paid to be in this book – these are very personal and heartfelt recommendations.

GROUP SUPPORT

Vistage
Vistage will help you become a better leader and will keep your company moving forward. Its proven leadership brings together executives from a diverse range of businesses and backgrounds to advise each other on how to make better decisions and achieve better results.

Tel: 01489 770200
Website: www.vistage.co.uk

Academy for Chief Executives

The Academy's Chief Executive Group is a place where successful CEOs and MDs meet to learn from each other, where their assumptions are tested, their ideas challenged and their dreams achieved. Leaders can inspire each other to excel, enjoy access to world-class speakers and develop leadership skills through professional one-to-one coaching, which provides a powerful mix of dynamic support for both personal and business success.

Tel: 0845 118 1028
Website: www.chiefexecutive.com

Institute of Directors

The IoD has long been recognised as an influential and respected membership organisation in the UK. With more than 100 years of success, the Institute is measured by its members, who are some of the most skilled and experienced business leaders in the country, representing the full business spectrum – from start-up entrepreneurs to directors in the public sector and CEOs of multinational organisations.

The IoD is a reputable source of relevant and accurate information on all aspects of business, and it takes its quality of service seriously. The last few years have proved a testing time for many businesses and individuals, underlining the importance of support – which sits at the core of the IoD's benefits and services.

Tel: 020 7766 8866
Website: www.iod.com

MD2MD

MD2MD will help your business to become more successful – by helping you, the person who has most influence on your business, to be the greatest leader you can be. With MD2MD you can learn from and with other leaders with real "university of life" experience. Members meet for one day each month, which is much more effective than lengthy business school leadership development programmes.

Tel: 01865 600 800
Website: www.md2md.co.uk

The Alternative Board

Imagine you had your own board of directors that provided you with direct access to outside experiences, objective advice and ongoing peer support to assist you in making better day-to-day and long-term decisions that would continually move your company forward. The Alternative Board makes this happen. This is an exclusive, membership-based organisation that helps business owners achieve more profitability, productivity and personal fulfilment.

Tel:	0800 118 5058
Website:	www.thealternativeboard.co.uk

MENTORING

Association of Business Mentors

ABM is the independent, not-for-profit professional body for enterprise and business mentors. Its purpose is to inspire and champion excellence in business mentoring, to advance awareness and standards in the business mentoring profession, and to make a sustainable difference to mentors and to the organisations and people that they help.

Tel:	07875 296155
Website:	www.associationofbusinessmentors.org

Rockstar

The Rockstar Mentoring Group is the UK's number one mentoring organisation for entrepreneurs looking to grow or raise finance. Their mission since 2007 has been to achieve measurable goals for businesses at the SME, established and start-up levels. They fast-track profit, growth and investment by providing experienced and successful mentors who have sold their own companies for an average of £18 million on a one-to-one, face-to-face basis.

Tel:	0845 652 2905
Website:	www.rockstargroup.co.uk

About the author

Jo Haigh is the senior partner in FDS Corporate Finance, a business she founded in 1989, with bases in London, Birmingham and Yorkshire, and a partner in FDS Knowledge, a specialist training and development business.

In 2012 and 2013 she started two new companies, Cracking Boards and Silver Exit.

Jo has bought and sold over 300 companies in the last 20 years, specialising in owner-managed companies, and is currently a non-executive director of six companies: Anchor Magnets Ltd, Sticky Content Ltd, TPD Corporate Finance, Imperative Training Ltd, Exact Business Taxation Services Ltd and Jermyn Consulting.

As well as being a regular presenter for the Institute of Directors on corporate governance and mergers and acquisitions, Jo is also a visiting fellow at the University of Leeds, where she delivers the corporate governance development programme for all academic staff wishing to hive off new companies, in addition to training and developing non-executive directors appointed to university companies whose role is to represent the university's interests.

Jo has received numerous awards and recognition for her services to business. In April 2013 she won the Non-executive Director of the Year Award for privately owned and private equity-backed companies in the Peel Hunt Non-executive Director Awards in conjunction with

The Sunday Times and the London Stock Exchange. She has also won the Outperformance Award for 2012 from Vistage, and has been IoD Business Adviser of the Year in 2006 and 2009. She has been a finalist in the CBI's First Women Awards and in the Sue Ryder Women of Achievement Awards, as well as being named as one of *Financial News*'s Top 100 Women in Finance and as Yorkshire Businesswoman of the Year, 2008.

She is a regular columnist on RealBusiness.co.uk and is the author of four previous books: the bestselling *Tales from the Glass Ceiling: A Survival Guide for Women in Business*; *The Business Rules: Protect Yourself and Your Company from over 100 Hidden Pitfalls*; *Buying and Selling a Business: An Entrepreneur's Guide*; and *FT Guide to Finance for Non-Financial Managers: The Numbers Game and How to Win It.*

Acknowledgements

No one can write a book like this without a huge amount of help, especially as I write mine out in long hand first, so I would like to say a special thank you to Arlene, my patient PA, and to Steph, my marketing director, for her help with coordination.

I would also like to thank my husband Mike, who read the whole manuscript to review my frivolous approach to grammar, and to my lovely editor Hugh for his words of encouragement and personal support.